HUMANISTIC NARRATIVES

ALSO AVAILABLE FROM BLOOMSBURY

The Five Senses, Michel Serres

Times of Crisis, Michel Serres

Rome, Michel Serres

Statues, Michel Serres

HUMANISTIC NARRATIVES

MICHEL SERRES

TRANSLATED BY RANDOLPH BURKS

BLOOMSBURY ACADEMIC
LONDON • NEW YORK • OXFORD • NEW DELHI • SYDNEY

BLOOMSBURY ACADEMIC
Bloomsbury Publishing Plc
50 Bedford Square, London, WC1B 3DP, UK
1385 Broadway, New York, NY 10018, USA
29 Earlsfort Terrace, Dublin 2, Ireland

BLOOMSBURY, BLOOMSBURY ACADEMIC and the Diana logo are trademarks of Bloomsbury Publishing Plc

First published in Great Britain 2025

First published in French as *Récits d'humanisme*

Cover design: Ben Anslow
Cover image © The Sorcerer, cave art. Sketch of Breuil's drawing. Photograph. Wellcome M0008769

A catalogue record for this book is available from the British Library.

A catalog record for this book is available from the Library of Congress.

ISBN: HB: 978-1-4742-8448-6
PB: 978-1-4742-8449-3
ePDF: 978-1-4742-8447-9
eBook: 978-1-4742-8450-9

Typeset by Deanta Global Publishing Services, Chennai, India
Printed and bound in Great Britain

To find out more about our authors and books visit www.bloomsbury.com and sign up for our newsletters.

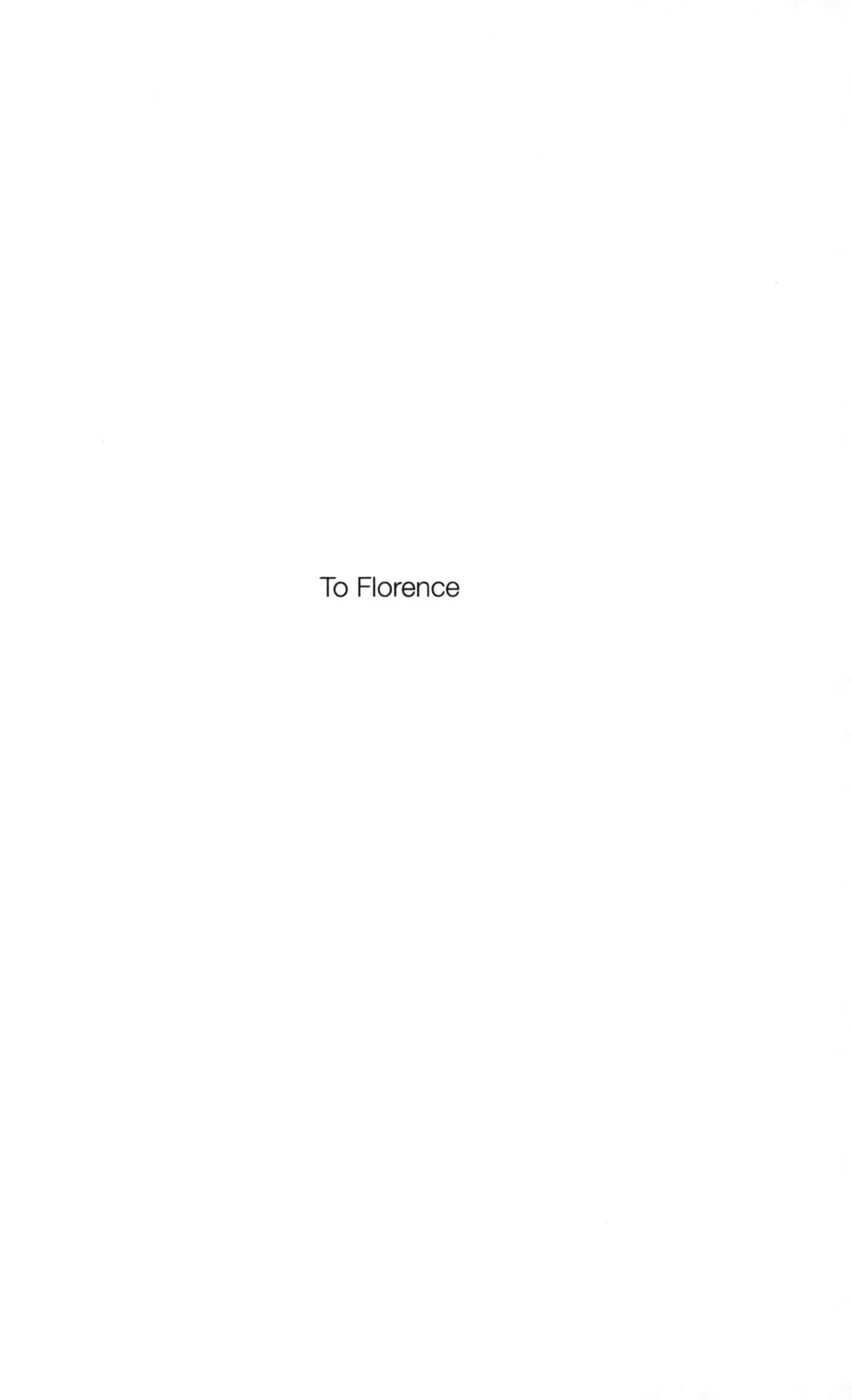

To Florence

CONTENTS

NOTE ON TEXT

This is the fourth and final volume of a series that began with *Hominescence.* Followed up by *The Incandescent* and *Branches,* this series has as its theme and could have as its title The Grand Narrative.

THREE FRAGMENTS OF THE GRAND NARRATIVE

Not far from the Isthmus of Suez, a hundred thousand years ago, at uncertain times and places, a tribe of Africans, attentive and lounging around a fire, were camping. Suddenly bringing endless palavers to a halt, a handful of them, exasperated, got up and decided to press on further towards the rising sun: to see, some of them said, for fun, the others didn't say, to ensure better hunting, the wisest ones claimed, to know, perhaps. Does one ever depart in numbers for a precise goal? The fiancée of one person, the mothers of several, the chiefs of the clan, the strict priests, tired old men . . . insisted that the birdbrains must return to them, if not that very evening, at least fairly quickly, so that the one person could make ready for his marriage and the others could assist the group with its ordinary life. In what language did they say farewell or goodbye to each other, and who, with pounding heart, shed what tears that morning?

I am shamelessly recounting what I don't know, for I don't know if people got married in those days, nor if they already put up with chiefs, nor at what age people died; thus, I can't say what wrinkles furrowed the faces of the elders. And did this tribe know how to light fire? Above all, straight ahead, can I even imagine the virgin spaces of a planet four billion years old, invaded by life for almost as long and yet humanless beyond this camp up until this particular departure? Can I depict this pathless earth, with untrampled plants, with fairly tame quadrupeds, an earth as dangerous and venomous as a rain forest, buzzing with multicoloured birds that settle and chirp on one's shoulders? Can I reopen, today, the universe that was open at that time?

So four-fifths of my narrative is swimming in the naive imaginary, but as for the rest, I affirm it with all the more certainty because we are all living today as the survivors of that inescapable episode, which can be called founding, since, through it, our explosive expansion began. Not a single human could exist in the rest of the world without this circumstance. Better yet, I shall recount the same primeval scene several times, which no one can now deny had to be repeated, here and there, at as many latitudes.

So, on that night, the little group disappeared from that isthmus between two seas, snatched from afar by the horizon: crazed adventurers, the easily excitable, the desperate, victims of sorrow or of scorn, passionate lovers that had been spurned, debtors, renegades, swindlers, murderers looking to hide their horrible secrets from those close to them, a few wiser and more mature adults, young people, mixed women and males lacking love, no old people. Seeing them leave without too many reasons and without themselves wanting to admit to being delighted about being rid of this contingent of hotheads, cumbersome to their authority, the chiefs, mothers and fiancées impatiently awaited, they said, their return.

Keep on sorting out, in this narrative, the numerous elements of a décor of convenience and those, rare and certain, for which, to the contrary, evidence abounds. In fact, this narrative's full truth depends on its scale of duration: neither human life nor history in the usual sense would be able to encompass it; to attain the conditions that would enable it to be recounted, they lack tens of thousands of years. Decipherers and readers of carbon-14, of a thousand fossils, of the genetic code . . ., we can only tell it today, a time when these means have placed us far enough back to observe, from this position, key moments, among which we find this one, behind circumstances covered over by forgetfulness, and therefore far enough back so that we can enjoy this tale, unheard of to the ears of our fathers.

Let's continue on with the rest of what happened. The adventurers were taking their time in returning. The others waited for them so long that they waited for them less. The old men died. Children were born who didn't have the slightest memory of this separation. The young women either got married or withered; chiefs succeeded one another, often making decisions that were so opposed to their predecessors that any continuity of tradition was lacking. A hopeless patience, first, and black forgetfulness, last, took hope's place. Earthquakes, struggles against predators and neighbouring tribes, the entire ordinariness of days, preoccupied the fraction the travellers had left.

There came a time when no one any longer gave any thought to those who had vanished without any reason at the horizon and whose tracks had been so erased by a hurricane the following week that, become lost, they never found, in the thick jungle, the way back. Did they really look for it, since each of them, or just about, would have refused to say to what extent this departure had lightened their collarbones?

Nothing is crueller than separation; nothing remains more in our consciousnesses, in the blackest black flesh of forgetfulness. Yet nothing vanishes as quickly from memories. The more difficult the thing, the more profound the amnesia. Do we remember our birth, our weaning, the childbirth when our little sister appeared? We only remember the less serious rendings. But we suffer from them in proportion to the depths, where the first rendings lie dozing, as burning, however, as the heart of the planet. My narrative does without the knowledge of a thousand details but is fed by this knowledge that's as certain and as universal as it is painful.

What became of these travellers to beyond the Sinai, who are as present and as lost as these memories? Since, today, we know the answer, gigantically long, to this question, we can finally pose it; better yet, we can finally recount the narrative of the peripeteia that gave rise to the question: forgotten by the Africans who stayed home, forgetful of Africa, their common cradle, their descendants populated Ireland and Japan, Karelia and Easter Island. We almost all live as the results of that decision. We shall return to this.

A few years ago, one fine evening, I found myself in a small plaza in the centre of Alice Springs, an Australian village in the middle of the outback, the only paleface among several poverty-stricken Aborigines, sprawling on the benches, drunk for the most part. The sun was going down; I didn't have anything better to do than watch them smile or poke fun at me. I remembered then a similar scene, more recent since it only dates back sixty thousand years, and which doubtless unfolded, at uncertain times and places, towards the far east of the Sunda Islands, in a fishing village in Timor or Tanimbar, on the Arafura Sea. Again, I am inventing this tiny hamlet from start to finish, those conical huts with the thatched roofs, those plankboard constructions above the lagoons, those long nets on the beach being mended by the women while waiting for the males to return to shore; smell the aroma of the fish the women are cooking; forget the fact that I know nothing about the junks on board which the people indigenous to these places and this epoch used to set sail; here they are, in front of you, going about their business, under the same short twilight.

But I can say, without any concern about being wrong, that a fraction of them, the morning of the following day, took to the sea, with or without any hope of returning, separating, perhaps without any valid reason, from their children and companions, from the group, with burning or light hearts, assured of their competence in regard to tides, hoping to reach, leeward, those coasts across the water that mirages sometimes revealed in a yellow glow above the horizon, and burning to discover there abundant food and easy women, kingdoms to capture, and ineffable paradises. Can I reopen, today, that sea that was open at that time?

I bet that the group was teeming with geniuses and pariahs, like the group that I could have said just now had left Egypt. That they reached the other side, this we know since they still live there: there they are, on the other side of the plaza, poverty-stricken, sprawling on the benches, drunk for the most part, all smiles. That they weren't ever able to return, this we also know since the fraction of the families – did families even exist at that time? – that stayed in the region never saw them again. Did the rise of the waters, a consequence of deglaciation, multiply the width of all the straits to the point of making them impracticable? Did the wind regime render the return crossing impossible? These wanderers certainly never found any happy valley or radiant city on the other shore, but, on the contrary, found desert, solitude, unknown animals that jumped instead of ran, giant crocodiles and venomous reptiles, seas poorly populated with fish but covered with translucent poisonous jellyfish, hunger, thirst, poverty, a senseless struggle to survive. Born into these hellish lands, without domesticable mammals, without grasses, where one only ate spines and insects, they learned at their expense that they had left the paradise lost without any hope of ever returning. And they forgot it the way they were forgotten.

Sixty thousand years later, victims of one of the most atrocious gulags in human history, the British convicts encountered, on the shores of the same Australia, these brothers in poverty and distress without recognizing them, not seeing them the way I saw them that evening, emerging from the fossil memories of the earth and of my consciousness; these convicts lived, anew, that same experience of famine and desperation. While history retains the memory of the suffering of these convicts, there is no such memory for the crossing of the sailors from Timor; I have just, for the first time, recounted their true adventure. As a result, I feel, deep inside me, the human dereliction of the Aborigines on the benches of that plaza cry out. They shout out their poverty and distress the way their sixty-time millenary ancestors did. As though the evolution that's the oldest in human time and the broadest in the space of the planet had already played, in certain privileged places, the scene that we sometimes happen to live in the little theatre of our relations as well as in the most remote mystery of our inwardness. Which of us has never wept over abandonment?

Always the same primal scene of separation; always the same crisis of memory and of forgetfulness; a scene and crisis temperate long ago, tropical there, and glacial here amid the wolves and bears.

As fascinated by the Northwest Passage as by the glaciers of Greenland and Spitsbergen, where, when I was young, I had contemplated the calving of icebergs from the navigation bridge for many hours, in the twinkling of an eye, I re-array my actors, just now from Africa or Sunda, in fox and sable furs; I put shoes on them made of seal skin; I smear their faces with fat extracted from a sea lion; I lean their backs forward in the face of the biting north wind; I suspend snow from their moustaches and eyebrows; I enclose them in their igloos on the pack ice; I send them to wander, hunt and fish with patience over the course of the single summer day, and so on. . . . If you don't believe anything about these details, most certainly kitsch, you can easily rest assured of the fundamental veracity of this third separation, shivering with cold and authenticity. A number of these proto-Eskimos drifted, by accident, on a floating island of broken-off ice across the strait today called Bering, with its violent currents that can't be reversed, and reached the cliffs of what we call Alaska. Can I reopen, today, those shores that were open at that time?

Land ho, land ho! They reached the shore without looking back; descending along the meridian, they sought milder zones, delighted to abandon those uninhabitable latitudes. This happened more recently, maybe fifteen little thousand years ago, might as well say yesterday morning, at uncertain times and places. Armed with harpoons made out of whale bones and daggers made out of walrus tusks, the women adorned with bear tooth necklaces (I am again amusingly inventing), this group slipped between the ocean and the continuous volcanic line formed by the Rockies and the Andes and, in multiplying, populated the new continent, as empty of humans as Australia or Eurasia was in the past. As from a horn of plenty, from top to bottom, Delawares, the Sioux of the plains, the Incas of the mountains, Toltecs, Aztecs, Fuegians, Araucanians . . . came out of these women.

Who, among the Chinese, Koreans or Siberians of the original shore, ever remembered these close cousins, who had sometimes reached the same continent on board pathetic rafts across the South Seas and just as quickly forgot their mothers and their lovers?

In sum: in Suez, between the Red Sea and the Mediterranean; on the Arafura littoral, wet and mild; between the Beringian ices, suddenly thickened by some new glacial episode . . ., a few contingent decisions, I mean sometimes made without reason, as though capriciously, initiated, crossroads by crossroads, the new human destiny. Coming out of the Kenyan rift and its wide region, in which we had lived stable (happy?) for millions of years, we set about wandering from here to there (disquieted?), occasionally suddenly changing direction: we spread everywhere. The human is recounted in travel narratives, interrupted with bifurcations. We have just lived through three.

But the scene recommences. Let's go back to the initial isthmus, or rather, let's leave it, for I am now of the party that has abandoned its tribe, which was settled in around its fire; this tribe will remain in the common African time, prodigiously originary. I am accompanying those fleeing, for I suspect that their group included my own ancestors and those of Poomena, born in Madras, a Brahman from a Dravidian family, a friend I liked to catch in ecstasy as soon as I came back after having, occupied by my affairs, abandoned her for a few moments. Had she already forgotten me? This happened several years ago. The fate of these adventurers concerns both of us and fascinates me as well.

I don't know how to calculate how many deaths the cost of this primal project conceived next to the fireplace on the isthmus amounted to. I even suppose that many departures of this type followed one another in order for one of them to finally succeed in the attempt. I am continuing to invent things, but at the end of a duration whose length I don't know how to estimate, one of these groups, surviving, reached a spot higher in latitude and farther east, certainly, where the same scene was reproduced, the circumstance certain, the times and places uncertain. In the Garden of Eden, in Jerusalem, on the road to Damascus, facing the Caucasus Mountains? I repeat, I know the essential of the matter; I don't know its modes. During the voyage preceding the decision to separate once again, whose duration can be estimated to be decades or, on the contrary, millennia, they couldn't have suspected that they would one day be called the Fathers of Eurasia. Two subgroups left one another, then and there, the one pulling towards the east and the other towards the west, and, as usual, forgot one another. Can I reopen, today, this fork that was open at that time?

Thus, dear Poomena, we abandoned one another, a hundred thousand years ago, your ancestors going, without realizing it, to populate Asia and particularly the southern shores of India, and mine becoming European and particularly of Guyenne. Don't give my narrative any scientific value; I am embroidering; I am telling tall stories; I am even claiming to stitch the oldest of all stories on to the newest by writing the grandest of humanistic narratives and that it brings the inevitable and matricial invariant to light: separation and forgetfulness, abandonment and dereliction, bitter decisions that sculpt existence. Thus, one can say that this narrative, even if half imaginary, is more decisive than philosophy and the sciences put together because in its nascent state, deep and continuous, it sheds light on the human. These successive bifurcations formed it within me more than the decisions said to be existential that I make myself and which, admittedly, do contribute to forming me, to creating my existence and to telling my narrative – the decisions being highly superficial, flying over my epidermis, the bifurcations being buried in the inmost depths of my genes. Yes, we never stopped departing, leaving one another, abandoning, abandoning one another, forgetting, forgetting one another, each of us pulling in our own direction, all the way up to that terminal and inaugural moment when, having marked the terraqueous space of the planet in front of itself with its toes and its hopes, with its tears and a few infamies, humanity returns back to itself. It never recognized itself as itself; it knows itself now. Sorry, I'm getting ahead of myself.

A thousand landscapes, now. Let's not forget, these humans lived in the world a hundred thousand times more and better than us, who have forgotten, as well, this wild space, today covered over, planed down, buried. Let's reopen, so as to better understand, what no one could call landscapes yet. With each obstacle (white-toothed mountains, Ararat or Damavand, glacial rock bars and barriers of ice, vertiginous passages in deep valleys, plains of an exhausting span, desert steppes full of spines, endless seas or lakes, dark woods, niches with untamable wild carnivores . . ., but also perhaps without any other barrier than their dirty rivalries, jealousies, appetite for power, deep-rooted hatreds, whether explosive or concealed . . .), each handful of humans sowed, in its wandering, the world expanse with its children, with its males and its women, lost. They sowed it with the very strong and the too weak: intrepid alpinists, tireless runners, inexhaustible swimmers, the men and women who could smell things from afar and who could see better in detail and the wide open; but also the women and men that were left, as though in a ditch, spurned lovers, mouths too numerous to feed, the abandoned elderly and nurslings, the sick and infirm gladly deserted in the woods, the imbeciles to whom infertile lands were left: slack lagoons, mangroves, hunting grounds without game, hopeless barren tundras. Humanity advanced by pushing aside madmen and convicts, by abandoning the corpses of the infirm and of the daring, even more than by conquering the world, as epics would have it. Fragility initiates. In these abandoned places, the weakest invented courage and technology. Precarity commands. When we found each other again, Poomena, we didn't yet know that we were behaving together like anciently abandoned survivors.

In bifurcating before these thousands of obstacles, these subgroups adapted to different environments and, like humans, did it with the help of what we call cultures. These humans began to drop like flies, very young, or, survivors, wandering, crossing . . ., began to often change languages and customs, tools and gestures, colours and habitats. They almost became like species within the same genus, except, of course, that they could still reproduce with each other, thus leaving to love the power of always being able to mend what abandonment had torn. I say species in the Darwinian style to pardon, as generously as can be, those who didn't recognize humankind in those they encountered across the open seas. But they didn't recognize it any better when they lived nearby. The old ideas certain philosophies in the recent West taught us, that man is a god to man or a wolf as well, say less about the adoration or the hatred we bear towards others than they show, in superabundance and in effect, that those who conceived these ideas contemplated the other, evidently, with eyes of a kind that immediately metamorphosed him or her into another species, whether divine or animal, as in the *Fables*. We have trouble considering each other fellow beings. If you talk well or jump high, I prejudge you to be an extraterrestrial, a mutant; poverty-stricken or smeared with brick, I see you as a devil or a dirty beast. I distance myself in both instances. I dispatch you to another class, not so much a social class as one from natural history. The difference of climates, torrid or glacial, the difference of foods, meat or fish, the difference of agricultural work or cynegetic exploits . . . made each of us a quasi-species unto ourselves. To these entirely natural causes, we add the passionate love we have for all separation: of class, order, hierarchy or judgement. Abandonment, for its part again, inspires us to rank or classify.

Thus, my dear Poomena, by means of heat or disesteem, because of rains or rites, you became, through time, a Dravidian and a motionless Brahman, dressed in a red sari from which sometimes, in the temple where you were praying without seeing them, the heifers would tear pieces to chew, at the risk of stripping you naked in the crowd. Thus, for my part, I became a Gascon, a peasant and a bargeman, a traveller and, a bit, a Franciscan; I began to write the way you loved to go into ecstasies. There isn't much we can do about it, but wouldn't you love, like me, to learn how our common mother lived during those distant times? If we recognized one another with such a tender ease less than ten years ago, don't you think that this feeling came from the tragic separation of our two parents, who may have died thousands of years ago, regretting their disunion? It seemed to me that we remembered this.

I also learned that your ancestors may have thrown themselves, starving, along the Coromandel littoral in order to dig the salt marshes and trade in salt, a good that's precious to everyone, but I never knew why mine, at least the ones I was acquainted with myself, found themselves thrown not far from the Atlantic littoral, in Gascony, on the banks of Garonne, where I was born. No one taught it to me, not my parents, embarked farmers, survivors of ignoble wars, nor the schoolteacher, who loved to hold forth nobly on killers like Napoleon or Foch, nor the village priest, who blessed the field and venerated Joan of Arc, horse, banner and helmet included, nor the entire history this lot drugged me with later, nor my classical culture, nor the philosophy of the widest scope: all of them too short. They taught me to think blinkered.

And I left, me too, during childhood, the Aquitanian paradise. Adieu. In my language, we say: *adischats*. I departed, they forgot me. They stayed, and I lost them from view. We abandoned each other by mutual fault, with the gentlest kindness in the world. I thought I was starting on my trip around the world at that time, while I was quite simply beginning my great voyage of return. Obviously, we must change the entire vocabulary that school, writing, history and culture have taught us. For each voyage where we think we are advancing is in fact returning or retracing its steps. The bush rangers, explorers and seadogs, the adventurers of every stripe as I dreamed of becoming, did nothing but return, turn around, take the road in the reverse direction along the immense duration of hominization. Vasco da Gama, Christopher Columbus, Marco Polo, Jacques Cartier, Samuel Champlain . . ., stars of the age of return.

Embarked in 1956 – admit, here, the derisory comedy of the date in relation to the scale of time from just now – for the Suez Canal and the Isthmus of Suez, did I know that I was returning, me too, on a small scale, to the places, as uncertain as the times, of a certain primeval scene whose wound I was carrying within myself like a thousand generations before me? On board, each of us, in his bunk, thought about the sea, war, politics, in brief, about the short history; some of us even, of which I was one, bowed, in the Red Sea, at the first sight of the Sinai, but who could think that he was carrying in his genes and his soul the forgotten memory of the first abandonment? What paltry martial or maritime occupations were we devoting ourselves to, while, beneath the weight of the pyramids and the shadow of sarcophagi, the land contained, buried even deeper, such secrets?

How many times have I thought about these primary scenes while flying over the Aleutian Islands or crossing the Australian Outback? I was finally returning. I was continually completing loops. I was no longer exploring the world, as my recent predecessors believed they were, but was tracing backwards the set of routes that a number of human generations had been travelling for scarcely a hundred thousand years. How has the West been able to allow itself to say, except out of boasting (merited sometimes), that it had boldly discovered every landscape of the Earth, when humanity in its entirety had already completed this loop tens of thousands of years ago? No, the West was going back to itself.

And I was returning, too. But school and writing, our histories and cultures were blinding our memories.

These thousand primeval scenes, where branchings begin to part and groups cut themselves off from each other, these decisive and repeated peripeteias, so varied in Kenyan walkers, island sailors or hunters from the pole, so diverse in wet climates or high latitudes, but so similar in abandonings, rendings and forgettings, better yet, identical, I repeat, in the fact that we feel emotional wrenching deep down in our consciousnesses, mustn't we double all these primeval scenes, for the sake of symmetry, with lived, multiple, often drawn, comically recounted, historically documented scenes of recent encounters in which the tragic is mixed with ridicule, cruelty with ignorance and arrogant assurance with foolishness?

So let's quit the long times that we have only been able to recount since recently so as to go back to the little duration already rewritten by history, that of my teachers and of our countries, even the microscopic duration of our singular lives, the fragments of common autobiographies I shared with Poomena. We have no trouble remembering those Portuguese or Basque pilots, those Dutch, French and English sailors, those European explorers . . . who landed in Africa, South America, India, the islands of Oceania, those naturalists who collected plants in the high steppes of Altiplano and Siberia, those colonizers of ten different stripes. . . . Yes, we remember them so well that they form a part of our educational adventure, a noble one, certainly, in that it encouraged visiting the universe and discovering its knowledge, but ignoble with bloody imperialism. During these three most recent centuries, extremely short, how did these learned men and these buccaneers behave towards the descendants of their own ancestors if not by responding to their advances with spit and musket fire? I want to substitute, for these all-too-well-known scenes of failed encounters, of unequal brawls, of incomprehension more than of tolerance and of pity, which I would prefer to forget, another common scene, a symmetrical one, which would bring this old history, so recent, to the complete stop that it deserves at the same time as kicking off in my own way the new narrative, the longest one, in which the behaviour would differ from these insults and these murders by the nascent remembrance of the vast duration that began with the exit from Africa and continues today.

So the new narrative I am inaugurating reattaches the long time to the era to come by leaping with both feet over history; such as we tell and read it, history only begins with human writings, while the Grand Narrative unfolds before our eyes as soon as we know how to decipher nature's writings, engraved on or in the cosmic microwave background, the brilliance of the stars, the weights of atoms, earth strata, fossils and molecules. Because we are starting to read, like an open book, in these silent things, whether inanimate or living, our contemporary time is becoming stitched to the time of these traces, which were illegible over the course of history; history opened up a crevasse that we have to cross.

On the upstream side of this divide, I have clumsily painted three more than probable variations on the primeval scenes of separation. Go follow a book whose narratives attempt to close this crevasse, to heal its wound, to close its parenthesis, to open up the hope for a new humanistic era, one connected to the Grand Narrative. In the meantime, I am now composing, on the downstream side, the final musical score of our reunion.

§

Listen now, repeated by every echo in the caves of the world, to the same rending cry, wept to varied musics: Why did you abandon me?

Why, having stayed on that side of the Sinai, did you forget about us while we were wandering in the desert between Egypt and the Promised Land? And why, travellers, did you desert your relatives on the other side of the isthmus? Why, fishermen of the warm shores of Timor, did you abandon your relatives shipwrecked by the deserts of spines, on the other side of the sea, to their starved fate? And why, settled into an exuberant plain of grass and bison, did you abandon your poverty-stricken brothers, prisoners of glacial regions? Why, stuffed with meats and grasses, didn't you run, on horseback, to deliver them from their igloos?

A long time had passed, as unrecountable as forgetfulness. As you know, the only thing that exists is what is said. Neither you nor me, nor anyone exists without reciting our existence, even in day-to-day life; one must recount oneself to be born; even a thing must be recounted for it to take place. No one could remember, and therefore could not recite, the three-faceted episode from just now because no connection existed between what we live now and what we lived a hundred thousand years ago. We hadn't built this bridge. Like children, we only disposed of short histories, without any tradition whitened by time. And these histories separated us, whereas this new bridge unites us. Since this narrative and its time are only being formed today, towards an upstream that was unimaginable yesterday, these things, finally recountable, are gently beginning to exist again. We read them in the sands and in DNA. Are we entering into an era of new novels, of new narratives and literatures, tales and dreams without which humanity would disappear? When we claimed to be recounting ourselves, over a mere several millennia, we were strengthening our separations, accentuating our abandonments; we were only reciting the local and the short, the European, the Asian, mere history. So who could say: humanity? Nobody. The global chronicle is finally being recited, starting from the African trunk towards branches that seemed diverse but whose graft we had forgotten. We can finally recount humanism.

Through this new bridging of these times, through this stitching between humanity's writing and that of things, we finally understand why you had abandoned us, why you had forgotten us to the point that you no longer recognized us when we found each other again, to the point that you didn't even consider us to be humans like you. And us, why did we abandon you? Why, crammed with knowledge, proud of our sciences, filled with culture, didn't we ever turn around enough to remember you? Today, the end of this ignorance is ringing; we can finally recount our primal separations; we can finally connect the time of our abandonments with that of our reunions.

Why did you abandon me?[1]

Listen afterwards, repeated by every echo in the caves of the world, to the same murmur of forgiveness, sung to varied musics: yes, I remember you.

I finally remember the era when we played together like brothers, when we hunted on the same lands, even if it meant quarreling heatedly at the moment we had to divide up the thigh and the hide of the same antelope. I especially remember the day and the hour, towards Sinai, in Timor or Beringia, when, with wrenched hearts, we separated from each other, when you left for the other side of the horizon, three times, content to leave me. I remember. I was standing, being brave, thinking I might collapse and sob. Over cruel minutes, I only saw your back, stiff, walking in a straight line without looking back. You have finally come back. I have waited for you a hundred thousand years; if it had been necessary, I would have waited for you thousands more. Come, I forgive you.

Forgive me, you too, for you knew, for your part, that I had cruelly abandoned you. Forsaken, forgotten. While you were leaving, you were waiting for me, your back stiff with anguish, to at least cry out your name once; you didn't hear any cry to come back. Thanks for coming back in the features of your great-

---

[1]In the preceding paragraph and the first full paragraph of this subsection, 'you' translates *vous*, the second person plural. The 'you' in this and the following three paragraphs translates to *tu* (or some other form of this pronoun), which is the informal second person singular. *Tu* is also used in the very first sentence of this subsection. I should furthermore point out that the 'you' in this and the following three paragraphs is female. All notes belong to the translator.

great-great . . . great-granddaughter, received by an equally multiply great-grandson. Come, abandon yourself; let me take you in my arms; I remember you. From now on, I will never stop remembering you. Have pity; remember me, too; I beg you, never stop remembering me. Don't ever leave me again. Let's write our common history on the sandstone of the cliffs and in the howlings of the wind and sing without surcease, to encode them into our souls and our genes, the unison of these two scenes; let's stitch these recent reunions to the separations that tore us apart in the past.

And what if we abandoned, again and in addition, the injustices we did to our fathers, I mean our fathers from recent history, a history rewritten with each generation in order to vindictively redress wrongs? No, let's not judge to be iniquitous and cruel those who formerly found each other to be monstrous because of the colour of their skin, because of the bearing and gestures of their bodies, because of strange customs prejudged to be barbarous. No, for we consider those men and women who abandon us to be monsters; we no longer recognize them; we see them as others. Transformed because already decided. Without realizing it, our near fathers, mine and yours as well, reproached the descendants of their mutual ancestors in this way, I mean by finding them to be strange, reproached, as I was saying, the descendants of their mutual ancestors for having cruelly abandoned their family: they reasoned correctly, all in all, and not wrongly as we had believed. Their despicable behaviour cried out, it too, but in a stupid language: why did we abandon each other? So let's include the cruelty of our fathers in our common forgivenesses. We cannot short-circuit history by taking up its resentments again.

Today, we forgive these first or primal scenes of universal human separation. We remember them, certain and identical everywhere and nonetheless variable, in the décor, the personages, the languages, the colours and the sounds, at uncertain times and places. Let's play, in fact and starting from today, the second scene. Let's reopen the universe that was open. We remember; we sing welcome and chant the encounters. Through these two acts, time changes: the long bridges the short. Let's reopen the duration of hominization.

Let's listen, sing, chant . . . I couldn't tell you how much I regret not composing music. I have just recounted these tears of abandonment, these cries of reunion, but have only tried to tell them, to write them, with silent ink, on mute paper, with the ear switched off, the soul saddened. The meaning blocks and interrupts these sounds; the sounds alone make the meanings melt together by traversing them. Worse, these narratives relate multiple separations, whose pretexts and reasons change, pretexts and reasons repeated over and over again in various languages, forgotten and hardly translatable into intelligible dialects today. And for the final encounters, multiplied a thousandfold thanks to these voyages, which I call voyages of return, heroic in the past and common today, have good translators ever been found? How are we to recount this narrative, a narrative that every ear on the earth would wish to hear, in several languages at the same time? How are we to say it in several voices?

Through music. Each language says a score of human music. We would need to make these laments be heard, as stretched out as tempests, as discrete as breezes, and these reunions, violent and tender like caresses of love. My narratives step over times that are longer than the lives of languages, recount circumstances that are factual, punctual, colourful, unpredictable, stage men and women, kitted out, dressed up hastily, who decide to go there or here without always having good reasons, on a momentary whim and contingently, the way we do every day and the way, in the navy, we used to cry out during the manoeuvres of bad moments, beneath the tempest: It's in God's hands! . . . I hear them cry in misery, shout with anger; the women wring their hands; lovers, male and female, risk suicide; listen to the adolescents moan. . . . These tear-stained narratives make us give up all hope of still working towards the vast personal, collective, universal, touching rhapsody of dereliction, but their untranslatable tonality still helps in understanding why our fathers, our histories, our cultures, tied to a language and, even worse, to writing, could not understand a thing when their ever so pale faces met with red ones or black ones, yellow ones or dark ones. Why didn't they listen to their drums, harps and horns? To hear these sobs better and to understand them together, we would have to be able to compose these tales simultaneously in every language, which, with their scores, would form a choir and orchestra, expressing abandonment and adventure, hope and rending, the interminable time of waiting and the contingent peripeteia, forgetfulness and memory, benevolence and cruelty, relentless pity . . . in an integral that would be inexpressible except in music. Even my screen, supposedly magic, doesn't help this heap, this dense polyphony. Only music . . .

So come to my aid, winds and winged creatures, muses, musicians; come, troubadours, divert this new narrative into sounds, the only project that matters for the humanity that's on the way to finding itself. Compose music to recompose humanity! Come help me, chaffinches and trade winds, nightingales and tramontanes, earthquakes and thunders, roars and tides, pentaphonic modes of the Bedouin, tom-toms in the Nigerian bush, monotonous chants of women veiled in black at Corsican funerals, trumpeters drunk with jazz in the bars of New Orleans, sophisticated harpsichords of Couperin and Rameau, background noise à la Xenakis, Beijing opera with its deafening percussion, gentle Balinese dances, Fauré's ecstatic *Requiem* . . . as well as what I heard, as an adult, from the Aborigines and, as a young sailor, from Breton bombards and Celtic bagpipes . . . so that this coherent chaos, this symphonic racket might accompany my visits to the beloved families stitched together by my life, as though my autobiography was orchestrating their particular scores, attempting to harmonize their differences, to whiten the colours of their linguistic kaleidoscope, as though the lightning-fast time of my existence could – oh miracle – project inside itself, as in a mirror, no, as in the sudden striking of a resounding cymbal, the longest time of hominization. No, no, don't truly believe that I'm travelling, that I'm exploring, that I'm pushing forward; no, I am only returning, finding again my most intimate friends, abandoned in the past, Poomena, my Dravidian sister, and my Aboriginal brother from Alice Springs, and others still who were deserted in the past and found again yesterday in Melbourne and in Florence, in Newfoundland and in Berry, in São Paolo and in the valleys of the Queyras, on the shores of the Pacific, of India and of the Cape of Good Hope, in Mali, Gascony, Djibouti . . . as though, far from a 'my home' that's so recent I'm almost ashamed of my homesickness, I was finally reconnecting fragments of answers to the pieces of questions asked by my ancestors, fossils of my language into the roots of theirs, a few fragments of melodies that could complete my unfinished sonatas; through a sudden concord, of a crazy complexity, I suddenly hear them conversing inside me, as though close to me; we are playing, here and now, in the same fragmented orchestra, the identical score of a polyphony that they can sign as well as I can. I hear the human within me well up in every language.

End of the overture.

I: SUBJECTIVE NARRATIVES

THE RETURN TO THE CRADLE

My fury turned into ecstasy. Standing in the waiting line, eager to see a ticket agent open up the window to check in for the twenty-hour flight from Paris to Cape Town, I saw an announcement light up: a twelve-hour delay. Anger, no, wonderment. The insomnia of the trip, normally nocturnal, changed, the following morning, into wide landscapes illuminated by the sun; from north to south, Africa marched past; after Garonne and the Pyrenees, then the smiling sea and the brownish Atlas Mountains, the Sahara unfolded its yellow dunes and, beneath the bend of the Niger, the rain forest displayed its green hell; once again, the temperate zone, then the Roaring Forties; I landed nourished by the food of the world. When will I cross the cradle-continent on foot?

The dinner that evening united several African writers, mostly English-speaking. Worried, all of them, about the often tragic states of their respective countries, they were looking for solutions, especially in education, which has priority and for the long term. As though suddenly drunk, I got up and recounted the African birth of humankind, the species' expansion into space, the Grand Narrative of the world and of the human race. Let's recount this narrative that's common to everyone, I said, to all the children and teach them, in bits and pieces, the sciences that produced it! Let's spread this narrative across the world, a synthesis of knowledge that's common to everyone! My friends stood up in turn, laughed and drank with me: let's celebrate, from the cradle onwards, universal education and the peace that will ensue.

All alone, I had visited the enchantment of the climates I wanted to travel, step by step. Over the course of the fraternal meal, we unanimously sang the new humanism. Over each mountain, sea, desert, city or hamlet, we saw a funnel cloud screwing around itself with its point downward that went about widening from the solitary individual, a pedestrian en route in his countryside, to the cultural communities that still cut up and constellate the planet, towards the circle lastly, with its centre everywhere and its circumference nowhere, of humanity, which stems from this continent.

Three stages of a rocket whose last module, good news, we finally know how to build.

Humanism

For up until today, humanism had never taken place because the universal humanity it evoked didn't exist. In a limited sense, this abstract word designated, during the Renaissance, the set of attempts, successful or miscarried, in favour of Latin letters first, and Greek letters afterwards. The development of scholasticism had strangled them; empiricist and logical, this philosophy, closed up inside the university, scorned the narratives of literature.

Dating from the seventeenth century and still enduring in Belgium and the English-speaking countries, the term 'humanities' covers these same Greek and Latin studies, whose leisure flourished in Europe long enough for rare evidence of them to still remain here and now. Will they be reborn in the West so as to rescue the dominant classes from ugliness and barbary, classes whose arrogant generations recently refused to pass on the mother wisdom of the Mediterranean to future generations?

Before this beauty collapsed, a few erudite Germans of the nineteenth century had designated by the word *Humanismus* a general doctrine and a pedagogy, both founded, in remembrance of the erudite men of the Renaissance and the philosophers of the eighteenth century, on what, since at least the Enlightenment, has blindly been called human nature. Who at that time had suspected that this conception was in fact imposing the customs of the West on all the inhabitants of the planet? There is even less risk that this humanism will be reborn than the other one; it either evoked universal humanity in this narcissistic and imperialist way, or it evoked it in an inaccessible manner: universal humanity therefore didn't take place.

It has just been born today and from an entirely different source. Derived from paleoanthropology, biochemistry and a few other disciplines expert in datings, the Grand Narrative, which recounts the emergence, expansion and adventurous voyages of *Homo sapiens*, allows us to draw the genealogical tree of a single and same family and therefore to attain a new universal.

And, once again, does a human nature exist? What then is humanity? Every answer proposed by the tradition to these two questions attempted to define our species in general. But some critics, ironic and judicious, would always object to each attempt with some animal said to be brute that would correspond to this definition, whether because it was a featherless biped or laughed, or because, an expert, it fabricated tools or made love face to face . . . . Ants, termites, beavers, chimpanzees, bonobos . . ., these are, as far as I know, so many political animals. And how many times, my soul, have you witnessed the reception of a diplomatic corps by a head of state or, when sick, the visit of a hospital department head walking in front of his retinue . . . without recognizing there, without fail, some male dingo dominating his females and other dependents, a rooster in majesty in the barnyard among hens and capons, a sea lion on the dirty beach, raising his flabby neck?

Ethology and genetics know how to measure this minute distance from our animal cousins.

Should one lastly define humanity as a thinking thing, how many of them have you encountered in the public square or some amphitheatre? Conversely, who can assure you that no animal has self-consciousness, that a cow in its meadow doesn't ponder over why it finds itself thrown, as it were, into this plot of alfalfa, ruminating on its dereliction? Which of us has ever entered into the coenesthesia of a bat?

Once these absurd definitions are rejected, once these modes of access to universal humanity are closed off, it seems easier to answer the question: Who are you, you, my fellow man, my neighbour, who I spend time with every day and think I know? To do this, I still commonly use concepts or adjectives, as when I was seeking above to define humanity as such: I judge her or him to be a criminal or an angel of goodness, generous or egotistical . . . . But those who condemn or praise in this way abundantly know that they themselves, sometimes celebrated for their gentleness, can, according to circumstances, become tigers and that fickle today, they can, tomorrow, be faithful. Composed of words or qualities in this way, these definitions, whether incorrect or unjust, err through a constancy that neither time nor life maintain. Lastly, by what right do we judge?

By what path, consequently, are we to encounter the other so as to finally do justice to his or her singularity? Living lovingly for more than fifty years next to a dear companion shows that truly attaining intimacy with another can remain a hopeless enterprise. This unpredictable gesture, that unpredictable word or some other unpredictable behaviour leads us to again ask the question: So who is she?

Obviously, we are asking it poorly. No doubt the question errs through the use of the verb 'to be': empty, formal, zerovalent and omnivalent at the same time, like the unknown *x* of algebra, a colourless white and the sum of all colours, the general equivalent of grammar and of philosophy, this verb only takes on meaning in becoming, in the passive, the auxiliary of another verb; 'being spurned', 'being loved', 'being accepted' or 'being driven away' are all better understood than 'being', period.

Better yet, over the course of our history, at least in its intelligent branch, every science, every field of knowledge, every practice, even medical practice . . . only developed to the point of effective operations on condition of abandoning the conjugation of this verb, I mean these logical definitions, the set of questions in the form of *what is*, questions that are formal, general, immobile, never falsifiable . . ., in short, on condition of abandoning being, essence, and even, maybe, existence, so as to enter into time and the ambiguous detail of the living.

A discourse on Being and an upper case substantivation of this lower case auxiliary, ontology, having a null and total range at the same time, therefore attains omnitude and nothingness, like the value of the verb it repeats ad nauseam, or only takes on meaning when united, like this verb, to acts, states or instances. At least ontology has the virtue, a sublime one by the way, of striving to assess the sum, the integral . . . (which are indispensable, no doubt, but inaccessible or absent) of every singular and landscaped being, of every narrative, piece of knowledge and literature. Where does the sudden swarming of these unexpected details come from?

Narratives of my life

From this. For the question concerning universal humanity, a genus or species that is unapproachable for the moment because it is too far away and perhaps non-existent, or concerning the other, quite close but difficult of access, even in love, I can substitute the query: Who am I, myself? To this question, as poorly asked as the preceding ones, antiquity answered by means of belongingnesses: I defined myself as citizen of Athens, slave or helot, participant in the Olympic Games, beneficiary of Roman law. . . . I was thus a part of a community, even if it meant casting the others out into the foreignness of Barbarism. We often, and still today, perpetuate this way of answering, we who are always intoxicated with a belongingness. For, formal in appearance, these definitions using the verb 'to be' most often conceal what I have called the libido of belongingness. Here, the question 'who am I?' signifies 'what group do I want to attach myself to?', 'what collective would I feel myself to be excluded from?' *Branches* told how, avoiding essence, logic or concepts in the Greek style, Saint Paul sought to tear us away from said divisions by answering the question by means of the pure identity *I* = *I*, outside of all society. But how are we to fill this empty and null formal equation, which describes personal ipseity (myself: *ipse*) by means of the, once again logical, principle of identity (the same: *idem*)?

To do this, Saint Paul, for his part again, as well as Saint Augustine and, after them, Montaigne, Rousseau, Chateaubriand and Stendhal, followed by a crowd of contemporaries, moved from logic to literature and recounted their lives, certain – like every passerby in the street – that a narrative, even a fragmentary one, says more and better than a definition. A definition is rigid, a narrative detailed; the first is stiff, the second flexible; the first is necessary, the second contingent so as to welcome circumstances; the one abstract and neglecting time, the other percolating in living duration; the one in the end false, due to confusion of the individual and the collective and thereby quickly unjust and racist, the other adapted, with exactitude and precision, to the singularity of the individual, to his changes of attitude, to the crossroads of his adventure, to the picturesque details of landscapes, themselves active in his encounters. Thus, the Acts of the Apostles, the Epistles of Saint Paul, the *Confessions*, *Reveries*,

Memoirs and autobiographies of those who followed swarm with a thousand narratives whose heroes describe and traverse hazards and misadventures, amid mountain trails and shipwrecks, sufferings, joys and despairs – all of them tribulations whose bushiness details the small change of the *self*. Today, I am celebrating the invention of this contingent form with as many delighted reasons as I did in the past for the invention of necessary geometry.

Popular, sometimes scorned, nevertheless supported by ten writers and as many philosophers, this custom of recounting one's life in minute detail in fact plunges deeper than abstractions and quintessences. Narrative wins out over the concept. Immersed in an environment and singular circumstances, some given event and the acts it leads to translate a character, betray it, reveal it, express it, and, behind this shifting profile and in keeping with this evocation, I see tendencies and colours, whereas a logico-ontological definition would have blurred the landscape of this soul, stiffened the contour of this face, darkened the hue of its personality, hidden the land it was traversing, lost the original time of its wandering hopes; since such a definition excludes contradiction, it doesn't comprehend any life: the saint sins, the hero is scared, the genius is mistaken and, in the same hour, I love you a little, a lot, passionately and not at all. Duration, plans, actions, situation and environment, emotions, desires and achievements, rich or rare relations, labours . . . enter into a narration, without beginning or end, as long as you live, without tail or head even, if you like: *ecce homo*. Affects and circumstances make gains over essence and existence, two concepts where the one is as abstract as the other. Who am I, who are you, who is he? The verb 'to be' digs a drain hole that empties every answer to any question into which this verb enters, whereas the tale of a life, even tiny, the life of some chosen other or my own, shy, weaves a kind of interlacing that stops this hole up.

Who am I? My life, an original time whose unfolding here and there, yesterday and now, is recounted, accompanied by walk-on actors, amid a varied land. So who am I? This tale, the detail of its stations (coups de théâtre and new developments), the aridity or leafiness of the land in which it unfolds, the extreme edge of its present in which the past, become necessary, suddenly plunges, like a tectonic plate, under the unpredictable contingency of the future. Who am I? This fleshy narration, its space and its time: this narrative and its landscape. Here, I find myself the hero of the story, a defined character of a certain literary genre, surreptitiously moving from being the actor of my life to the role of being an actor in my representation. Yes, the question 'who am I?' receives a better answer in a narrative than in a definition, in literature than in logic or ontology. Unless the latter, far from scorning the former, gives it its letters of credence and testifies to its profundity. For a long time, I have declared that only philosophy can demonstrate that literature says things that are more profound than the things philosophy seeks to demonstrate.

Nourished by the humanities from a tender age, we took pleasure in reading Plutarch's *Lives* not only because this book of parallel lives established connections between two destinies but also due to the interest that attached us to these illustrious examples. We loved Romulus and Theseus; we love them less, but we still adulate champions, whose lives attain narrative all the more easily because their feats astonish. Those who take them as examples agglomerate their mimetism in order to, fascinated, hear them recount. Their publicity constitutes the public. Thus, we devour the sports journals or the movie magazines because champions and stars incarnate beauty, strength, vice or virtue, in short, an achievement; their lives carry it out and seem to have a goal; their lives have a head and a tail, a direction, a beginning and an end. A talent striving towards a target gives their existence a kind of unity or literary line, at least the sustained character of a song or an incantation.

So who am I? The champion I admire and imitate, star of my inward theatre, hero of my private narrative; I take myself to be such in my cinema: certainly, I can see myself in Hamlet, in his confidant or in the palace groom; my absence of destiny imitates these examples or another non-example who recounts his anti-Memoirs. Supposing I fail at becoming my own champion, at least I have the choice of my preferred star, of my preferred singer, of my preferred football player . . . an athlete, of my Hercules, a sailor, of my Ulysses . . . who would serve as my models and whom I can imitate. I recount my life by proxy. The *we* has replaced the *I*, which has vanished. For the ancients, the person was frozen in a theatre mask.

Who am I? The hero I play on my own stage? Even when apathetic, I incessantly recount my daily acts to myself; I tell myself my gestures and my attitudes, my work and my rests; I eat, walk, think, play . . . and recite it to myself; I love and, in good instances, we recount it to ourselves. The most faithfully in the world, the most clearly too: do I know how to live, can I act, feel, cry . . . without ever confessing it to myself, without weaving a veil of silent language in the middle of my affects and my decisions? Don't sleep's dreams, in the absence of clear consciousness, simply continue this irrepressible narrative by other means? The child impelled, before going to sleep, by the fear of being alone in the night to beg his mother to tell him another story always lives inside us. Don't leave me, tell a different dream than the one whose colours will calm or terrorize my shadows. Narrative accompanies anxiety and sometimes erases it; hardly discursive, its sequence delights me with myself and covers over the black fear, whose terror chokes me, of falling into the nothingness. I incessantly recount myself in order not to collapse into sobbing. The coauthor of the subject, this recounted story builds a guardrail that protects it from the void. Thus I live and tell double, the less unhappy author of a tale, of a continuous incantation, which are audible, sayable, meaningful . . ., or the silent actor of unmatching, panic-stricken behaviours when I no longer manage to distance these behaviours in narrative, whose global bond strongly resembles what I call *me*. In order that I may call it, I must indeed speak. This latent discourse puts binder into my actions and the tatters of trees and streets in which my gestures and labours are lodged. How?

At the beginning, background noise

By a process I understand poorly, but which I want to try to describe, despite the clumsiness with which, familiar with the cognitive exit and dazzling objectivizations, I climb down the introspective descent – I dive into myself, eyes closed, solitary, mute, converted, attentive. With difficulty, I reach a low bedrock, underneath memories, emotions or affects, where my coenesthesia feels, directly and free of language, the vital heat. I would pass out from cold if it were absent; ice kills; we die from shivering. Burning, my body dives and swims in a warm fog. Even across the silence of health, I believe I perceive, emanating from these disordered living sparks, a kind of hubbub that resembles, in some way, the ringing in the ears whose vibrating expanse has assailed me for years, an uproar probably issuing from the effervescence produced by the admirable network of nerves and vessels, by the exchanges of energy the organs, tissues and cells are devoted to, according to billions of biochemical programmes. From the Brownian motion of this lively heat, a chaotic background noise emerges, discontinuous and continuous, whose primal murmurings, warm, emit the originary cries, calls and meaningless clamours of inwardness, at the limits of the inaudible. Can I name this muffled hubbub, in which temperature transforms into acoustic cloud, unconsciousness?

Breaking surf, cataracts and turbulences densely woven like the braids of hair a river ties and undoes at the exit from a dam or a bridge produce this white noise, always fluid in some way, granulous like a cascade, continuous like a torrent. In the thorax and under the diaphragm, a lake of tears sleeps, wakes, roars like the lava of a volcano and pours out in a stream of sobs. The processual of internal time flows, beats like blood, boils like tears. Liquefied by this inferno, the primitive psychic energy wells up, gushes forth, pours out, streams forth, deplores, never stops crying; laments, childish, adolescent, adult, wise, standing, *stabat mater dolorosa, juxta crucem lacrymosa*;[1] weeps – bent over, aged, on the verge of passing away – before the vanishing life; cries day and night, wide-awake, across sleep, in acts and through thought, amid solitude and the entreaty offered to others, turned away, misled, within an inch of being annihilated, found again, welcomed; cries, alone, lost in the crowd; laments before the history in decline of collectives on the way to making themselves into animals again; ends up crying, lost, distraught, before God, whose absence infinitely adds up the tears of joy and the tears of sadness, the integral of cheerful and pathetic loves, as it were. Fluid unconsciousness noises forth.

From this background noise made by waterfalls, windmills and the sea, by the living body and the silent soul, signals then emanate, like waves, high and long, formed I don't know how, on this sea of murmuring. The secret relationship between these pointed signs and the meaningless fluctuations from which they spurt forth makes one feel pleasure and pain, round comfort or sharp spines; not some defined enjoyment or suffering, but the basic discomfort or comfort, the fundamental tonality of my relationship to the body, to life and to time, in which I recognize that gushing forth that, later and higher, is going to pervade all my acts, all my emotions, all my words with its consonances of harmony or its pathetic dissonances, which are already established there, in accord or discord. An old man of elation, a child of melancholy, a man of sorrow, a girl of jubilation. My basic joy exceeds the cataract of tears.

---

[1]The first line of the hymn *Stabat Mater*, a hymn to Mary: the sorrowful mother was standing next to the Cross, weeping.

Sometimes, from this chaotic confusion and its fluctuations, at the edge of my 'consciousness', from this background noise and these minute signals, which are imperceptibly sharp, a fragment of a tentative melody, unheard of and coming to hearing, can surge up: ululation, lamentation, hymn, cantilena, plaint, monotonous chant. . . . This melody makes me cry or rouses me with tenderness. I desperately keep my inner and outer ears open to hear its birth. Should I succeed in this, it will begin to cover over with its melodic line everything that preceded and conditioned it, the summits of signals, the random chaos of murmurings, the disorder and hubbub. In its nascent state, its tentative continuity smooths the spines and orders the chaos. A beginnings of an inward landscape integrates the scattered elements that come from the heat the way the outer landscape unites the trees and peaks of the environment into a painting.

A musical emergence starting from a thousand clamours. It mewls like a newborn, doesn't bawl, but almost silently gropes along its way. Along its voice. A miracle: the birth, now, of the 'voice of consciousness'. It speaks. No, it prattles, babbles, stutters, stammers, speech without words, language without tongue. Starting from the primitive music, emanating itself from the noise, a beginnings of articulation muffledly seeks something of the meaningful. Already, a kind of sense, at least directional, had surged up from the senseless when the monotonous chant enveloped, with its long line, the scattered and broken rocks of the hubbub, a still disarticulated meaning.[2] But, gradually, a few consonants break up the voice only chanting vowels, and now the first scraps

---

[2]Sense = *sens*; senseless = *insensé*. *Sens* would normally be translated as 'meaning' here, but the French word can also mean direction, a meaning Serres invokes, so I have resorted to 'sense', appealing to its less common additional meaning of directionality. In the rest of this work, I have rendered it as 'meaning'. *Sensé* (which is also used in this paragraph) and *insensé* normally mean, respectively, sensible and not sensible or reasonable and unreasonable, but here Serres is taking the words in their etymological sense, which is, of course, meaning. So, in this work, I have

of what I was calling narrative appear, a narrative that, in return again, integrates, erases and conceals everything that preceded. Sovereign, this narrative envelops, with its meaning, the in-order music and the disordered noise, both of them meaningless.

Language doesn't know how to say its birth

I myself, in the preceding pages, have had to resort to language to describe its non-discursive antecedents, foundations I have therefore betrayed so greatly that, like Orpheus, the cithara player of old, I risk or merit having my darling Eurydice leave me and return back to the place from which I had arrogantly believed I could pull her. I have committed the crime of turning around upstream of language, towards music, upstream of music, towards signs, upstream of signals, towards the background noise, upstream of the originary hubbub, towards the flames of the organs of life. One doesn't easily climb back up from this underworld, from embers and ashes. Orpheus descended, like me, towards the foundations of his art, immersing himself in the black box from which language emanates and the *self* surges up; he had hoped to pull up from there the woman he loved more than himself, more than his own flesh, his life or his meaning. With the sound of his lyre, he led her out of the shadow; since he turned around to see her, she disappeared. If I speak, if I recite . . . I will no longer hear the music or the noise at the sources of speech, of narrative, of the *I*.

A four-stage rocket launches the birth of language, the emergence of the *ego*, and the dawn of narrative, which, in recounting them,

---

translated *sensé* as 'meaningful' and *insensé* as 'meaningless', except – regarding the latter – in this particular sentence.

forms them, creates them, but forgets their beginnings: this rocket wells up from heat, first towards the white noise; from this hubbub, it moves to the first signals; then from these to tentative melodies; lastly from the latter to the first vowels . . . Noise, cry, chant, music, voice . . . precede the basic utterance, before the language of narrative. The musical offering launches language, which recounts. Language doesn't know how to say its chaotic and musical birth; can music sing the noise from which it is born? In this underground, Orpheus precedes the writer. Their slow deliverance after their dive down reveals something of the universal, already: heat, disorder, background noise, meaningless musical plaint, phenomena that are just as much external as internal. If all meaning describes a particularity, here lie universals before meaning.

A paradox: individuation takes place, heatedly, at this quasi-physical level. Individuation proceeds by creating a chain, whether musical or articulated as a narrative, whose sequence is made of time. More or less long, less or more continuous, this envelope links prior chaotic groupings of the meaningless murmurings. I hear this time as music; I grasp its duration as narrative. Time and duration are born in the passage from disorder to order or through a mixture of order with disorder, when packets of noise coexist with a few sustained signals, when instants cut up like atoms mix with stretched-out moments. Time and duration, which are said to be so difficult to decompose, are easily divided since they are composed – I don't know how – of tension and dispersal, memory and forgetfulness, weaving and holes, like filters. Like the *ego*, music and narrative, time appears when scattered pieces and a linking are – I don't know how – added together, when continuity and discontinuity are strangely mixed, when they are mingled, filtered and therefore percolate. Individuation begins by differentiating itself via the fineness of this mixture and the speed of its sequence. It is born, original, from the precise threshold of this percolation. I become a mixture of retentions and absences, of attachments and oversights, of attention and letting-go.

Most of all, this *tempo* characterizes individuals and can separate them when one person lives *allegro* and the other *andante*. Above all, I last, rhythmical. I exist as the figures of my rhythm. Rather fast, I admire those who are slow. The concord of two lovers is reckoned better in tempos than in music; even and odd time signatures are lacking. Our fundamental relationship to life and the body, whether one of concord or of discordance, follows this internal constitution of time, a constitution forged in the innermost heat of the organism's energy exchanges. The irreducible singularity of my relation to duration is understood to be an original relationship of discontinuous instants with moments of continuity. I abandon myself to the tempo, and irrational besides, of cadences.

Of course, the chain of my DNA, the arrangement and functioning of my neurons, the software programmed in my muscles and joints are already so many individuations. But the internal operation called my consciousness comes out of these given groupings in order to forge itself actively, always in real time. Or rather, it constructs my time according to these fragile mixtures. I think I first hear a kind of voice, a murmuring emerging from an indistinct sea rumbling. I can only name this murmuring my *self*. Before comprehending myself, before knowing, I hear myself. Everyday French says this wonderfully when it asks *comment je m'appelle* [what I am called; literally, how I call myself]. In fact, I hear a call only addressed to me, and an echo answers as though under a solitary, empty and sonorous vault where I would cry out, anxious, *is anybody there?* and where answers would stream from the walls and arches of the ceiling: *there, there, there . . .*, a new rumble. This echo and its call – I call myself – individuate, through a tied together sequence, the person who transmits, repeats and hears it. A discontinuous continuous circle of the mouth and the ear, of the transmission and the reception, a feedback and envelopment of the plaint and the listening, of the cry and the hearing, an internal reciprocal feeding engendering individuation through the consciousness of time.

The *re-* of the words *récit* [narrative], relating, recounting, reporting . . . expresses and repeats this fold.

The time of mixtures

Continuous because it arises from attention and is preserved in memory, time or the processual of duration is constructed – intentional, voluntary, stretched tight; here, time is named on the basis of tension, the tension consciousness adopts to perceive itself. Quite the contrary, immediate and free consciousness, slack, only perceives the discontinuous; the time given in this way, if I may, is presented in shreds, tatters, scattered limbs; it leaps, quantum. When I spend an hour dreaming, I jump without any transition from a long memory to an overwhelming emotion, from a slowly attentive tenderness to some brief resentment, from a prolonged erotic fantasy to a fine and flashing intuition . . . Time is named on the basis of the cut, understood in the sense of an axe, but also the way we say a drug is continually cut with some filler. Linguists hesitate between two Greek roots for the word: *τείνω*, *teinō*, to stretch out, or τέμνω, *temno*, to cut. Far from hesitating, add them together. These same linguists are surprised that 'rhythm' comes from the Greek word signifying to flow, whereas, precisely, rhythm cuts duration up into measurements. Don't be surprised, add the two senses together. Precisely designated by our language, this composition between the continuous and the discontinuous expresses the nature of time and the duration of internal consciousness at the same time. How can this sum, composed of opposites, occur?

When, perchance, something sustained emerges starting from the discrete: then real time comes about, mixed – I don't know how – from the stretched-out, the retained and the broken, from its two roots in some way; then music comes about, a melody sustained, likewise, by means of notes and granular cries; then narrative comes about, in which my voice, broken with consonants, is linked together with vowels; then history comes about, that fabric of meaning stemming from selected events; then the Grand Narrative comes about, from the binding material of numbers and atomic particles, from the weaving life of molecules, from the human recounted starting from highly rare fossils. . . . The Universe, life, me, us, even humanity are born from a continuity, singular each time, that shoots up from the basic discontinuity, mixes with it, composes itself into it, integrates itself into it – how, I don't know, but I shall seek the answer. Other linguists confess that the temperate mixtures of temperature and temperament explain the word *temps* [time] marvellously.[3] It mixes the two Greek roots from just now, the discontinuous root and the continuous one, like 'rhythm'. Thus the word *temps* describes time perfectly, the time of my consciousness as well as the time of bad weather [*intempéries*] (my soul unfurls itself as a landscape granularly sunny beneath the rain in sheets and drops), the stochastic time of history as well as the Grand Narrative of the Universe, of life and of humankind, according to the progressive expansion of scale this book is going to follow.

It is a unitary time because it is mixed in this way.

Ills

What would happen if I ceased recounting my life to myself, if I stopped crying it out, deploring it, lamenting it, singing it, representing it, telling it? Like Eurydice, it would vanish, without shelter, fall back into tatters, collapse into the hell of noise, towards the hubbub and furore, a black hole of disorder and discontinuity. This has often happened to me. Life fell into pieces, into vociferations, into

---

[3] *Temps* can mean time as well as weather.

pebbles of background noise as soon as I could no longer recite it to myself, as soon as the music went silent, as its melody didn't rise up, as the continuity didn't gel. Narrative, then, dashed far away from me. Peace deserted me; my loves abandoned me and left me torn apart into scattered limbs; health forsook me; my work ran aground, thought quit me . . . Misfortune, disease, violence, abandonment, ills in general, physical, mental, moral . . . cut life up into pieces, a life become meaningless because they destroy its narrative. It became unrecountable. Since the miserable person can no longer set forth his own life, he recites to himself, in place of his own, the life of some cardboard hero, like that killer Napoleon, no longer a model, but rather a substitute.

No more subject, no more substance, only substitutes. Substitution is the main operation of the theatre (the actor plays in place of the character, and the spectator identifies with the former) and of illness, whether mental or other, which I just talked about. Perish the two thoughts of minimizing theatre by relating it to pathology or of weakening the latter by comparing it to theatre. No, representation and illness converge when, tired or weak, we substitute stories and borrowed landscapes for the autonomous narratives of our lives.

Seen or heard continuously, noise, speech, music and media images steal the aforementioned voice of consciousness, the body's tonus and the landscapes we could have created of ourselves. Such media steal souls and recreate them in their image. They abduct them upon the very birth of their sound. Now deaf to his own voice, some person no longer hears, like a dog, anything but the voice of his master. Right where the theatre used to, at rare and select occasions, construct a collective soul, the continuity of the spectacle eradicates singular souls at their source. The expansion of stupidity here presents less danger than the major sociopolitical risk incurred globally by this destruction of the personal *ego* and of its own narrative in favour of a collective formatted in a pathological and totalitarian manner. The media drug risks putting the sick and slaves in chains. It forces us to descend into a conventional and fitted-out underworld.

With more or less strong tremors, sometimes more violent than the first one, aftershocks follow earthquakes. Quakes don't last two or three murderous minutes, as is believed, but three or four weeks. At the time of the 7.2 Loma Prieta quake in the fall of 1989, we underwent at least ten aftershocks of around 5.0 or 6.0, not counting the gentle ones that caused the walls to tremble and gave a slight vertigo.

So one morning, at dawn, I opened the windows and, surprised, heard the birds singing among the branches. For twenty days, I hadn't perceived the air's taciturnity. I didn't remember when nature began to fall silent either, at 5.04 pm on 17 October or before the first shock? We didn't realize that we were surviving in a silence punctuated by telluric aftershocks.

A landscape of thickets and leafy high forests, my soul normally resounded with chattering magpies, whistling blackbirds, cawing crows, nightingales and chickadees among the moaning breeze and the cracking branches – murmurs, breaths and voices. This continuous hubbub would prepare, as background noise, the incantation and narrative of my life, its abstract or concrete text. Following an earthquake, all this nature fell silent. Music and language left me.

I opened the window that morning, and then, a marvel, there were chickadees and magpies returning with winged swiftness, complaining blackbirds, baritone crows, nightingales drunk with musical runs, plus the breeze grazing the grasses and the twigs crushed by my steps. The dove with the branch was announcing the conclusion of the flood; upstream, over the primal waters, the hubbub the Bible said preceded the breath (the word that created the world) had returned. Does the Bible tell the beginning of the Universe, or, better yet, that of language and of my soul?

The way earthquakes destroy external landscapes, accidents, illnesses and sufferings interrupt the subterranean work that conditions narrative, whose melodic line resumes with the ebbing of the waters, in the happiness of the organs, with the calming of the earth, with the end of the aftershocks, with the blessed return of the beloved one. Pain and hatred, of others, of the world and of oneself, cause the narrative to fall silent, the way earthquakes extinguish birdsong. How can one recognize suffering and Evil?[4] By the stopping of the narrative, by the stifling of the song, by the blinding of the landscape: the movement of the story breaks off, as well as the line of the incantation; the sea noise fades away. By the shrinking of our life down to its acts, distinct, and its actor, isolated. By the disappearance of the author. We can resurrect him to compose, sing, recite, recount . . . after hatred and pain have ceased exerting their hold: only then do we augment our life ('to augment', the word 'author' comes from this verb) up to the narrative of our survival. Victor over pains and resentment, the narrative, thus recreated, can create, in its turn and as though in return, the soul itself from which it came. The devil doesn't create, but rather prevents the word, divine creator, which, under the hold of misfortune, enters into a great silence.

Augmenting

Starting from the elementary biochemical level, from the living fire, psychic energy is created; this latter doesn't resemble physical energy in any way; contrary to the two laws that regulate physical

---

[4]Evil = *Mal*, which I translated as 'ill' earlier in this subsection in an effort to maintain the double meaning of illness and evil found in the French word.

energy, psychic energy is created to be spent. We discover our capacity to achieve some task, difficult enough to require strength we seem to lack, only when pressed to act, when we force ourselves to undertake it, as though this decision even recruited its conditions, outside of all hope. Such a collection, unexpected, used to be thought of as the grace of God's help in difficult situations, as though one received a gratuitous gift just when one needed it. Before testing our strength, we never truly know what we are capable of, nor the capacity of our body, even less what our inventiveness is worth. The more I run, the more I walk or swim, the better I swim, run and walk. I work and think all the more and all the better for thinking and working. Training finds or invents its own resources, sometimes unexpected, and creates its own conditions. We find ourselves sources of unexpected resources.

Does the fact that the vital heat changes into noise, music and beginnings of language reverse the increase of entropy? Within metabolism, can the transition between ordinary energy, that of sugars and phosphates, and information, equivalent to negentropy, explain this inversion of the rules concerning the normal exhaustion or the vital resurgence of energy? Living energy, in a way, reveals itself to be inexhaustible: the secret of our creations?

At the most, the more one freely spends one's reserves, the more one becomes rich from this. I resemble a genetic source more than a data bank. Oh, my animated language, so did you know that you were capable of perpetual motion? So I am going to lead you to right where you have long been afraid to go. I am creating my endless narrative.

At the least, when I fall to the depths of misery, I experience a resource, a new boost, a mysterious gushing forth whose power sometimes impels me out of the well, streaming with tears, convinced of despair, shouting out with new life. Desperate, certainly, but my narrative will resume.

Genres of narratives

We all need a narrative to exist. In search of the *I*, worse yet, of the *I am*, Descartes told how, as a soldier in Germany, he took refuge during a cold spell in a room warmed by a stove, a source of heat, in which he received a visit from the Evil Genius, an unbeatable deceiver, and the fearsome struggle he engaged in against its falsifications, a battle from which he exited as victor only with the help of God, omniscient and all-powerful. The philosopher made this smoking success be taken as a *Meditation* of truth, whereas it was a matter, quite simply, of a narrative, and of a narrative, quite precisely, in which the fire burns in an enclosed area and in which the Evil could destroy everything, even the possibility of speaking. The Cartesian *ego* shoots up from a breathless suspense: Who is going to win, the devil or the Good Lord? Or rather: without the story of this heated and a little too blustering quarrel, would we have seen this *I* be born as a stake of these powers?

Without Saint Paul's vision on the road to Damascus, without his long silence and the torrent of words that followed, without the novel that was the Acts of the Apostles and the narrated adventures (the stealth descent along the city wall at the bottom of a basket, imprisonments and shipwreck), without the conversion of Saint Augustine, without the *Confessions* that recounted it . . ., would the modern and individual subject have emerged? The *I* surges up from autobiography.

We all need a narrative to exist. What genre of narrative? Religious in Genesis, in which the lives of Isaac, Jacob and Joseph . . . are unfolded, epic with Achilles's exploits, furious beneath the walls of Troy, tragic in Oedipus's tribulations, historical under Pericles, poetic with Philemon and Baucis's hovel, holy in the Gospels, comic thanks to Sancho Panza's proverbs, freely multiple by the grace of Jacques the Fatalist, melancholic for Emma Bovary, solitary, almost paranoiac under the inspiration of Rousseau or Chateaubriand . . ., each of these personages, recounted or recounting, embraces what the tradition calls a literary genre . . ., as though literature, through these types, said some individual from this or that angle or sometimes painted a shifting, ambiguous, living silhouette, whereas the abstract definitions I was talking about earlier exhaust themselves in drawing or formalizing an absent, inaccessible and inflexible sketch of him.

We all need a narrative to exist. But what genre of narrative should we choose? While, perched on a gable, trowel in hand, I am clumsily doing masonry work on it, I can recount to myself or to you that, skilled, I am smoothing a joint between two stones, that, heroic, I am exposing myself to the danger of falling or, vain, parading myself for no reason before the view of the neighbourhood, that, prudent, I am sheltering my family, gymnast, getting exercise or building, mystical, my children's habitat, the way others raised their cathedrals. I can relate my life to you and myself in these ten ways, exaggerated, deceitful, humble, derisory, drily factual. I change, choose, bifurcate; my soul metamorphoses. Ten possible narratives of my activity unfold according to the literary genres: the home repair manual, the epic song, the collection of poetry, the novel, tragedy, comedy, performance, theatre. . . . And what if the aforementioned genres summarized the ethical intentions of our lives or, as we shall see, the moralities in fashion during the eras of their flowering?

I love to vary my narrative: this morning, I see myself as the hero of a novel, tomorrow, as a ridiculous comic; I have known myself to be more or less courageous in risky situations, sorrowful in tragic passions. . . . In defiance of the rules, my narrative mixes genres. Autobiographies often relate conversions, Claudel's or even Proust's. Kierkegaard recounts that he went through three stages, aesthetic, ethical and religious. Our lives have all the more meanings because they change them. What stupid role did I play here or elsewhere?

What personage did I display during those occasions? Thus, these genres play the role of reference points. Of course, we see them as being separated, but the adventurous duration of existence haunts them by turns. The narrative of life navigates by taking its bearings according to these seamarks, by using tools available in these stores that are open to everyone. It chooses between the heresies (αἵρεσις [hairesis], in Greek, means choice) arrayed on the shelves.

We all need a narrative to exist. In any case, no one loves his life if he doesn't recount it to himself; life is better when it is easily transmuted into an original narration. Will I be calling myself a liar if I borrow a role from the store rather than playing my own role, rather than composing my musical score? How exactly am I to genuinely attain my own role? Let's not misunderstand the word 'narrative'. In an ancient or classical sense, it designated the statement of a series of events linked by the usual time of the sun, of genealogy, of the watch or a calendar, sometimes interrupted, to maintain interest, with unexpected coups de théâtre. Thus the Homeric poems tell of the bloody exploits of Achilles and of the adventures of Ulysses across unknown seas and lands; thus Flaubert related the great sufferings and little betrayals of Emma Bovary. Anyone can imitate this heroine, this hero, this traveller, can substitute himself for this incarnation of the canons of his culture, can choose his heresy. By means of genres and champions, literatures thus open up shelves on which an *ego* and a life by proxy – mediocre at leisure or, according to your choice, grandiose – can be procured.

As said literary genres progress in approaching singular individuals and their ambiguous inwardness, or as they progress in exploring the resources of language, they gradually leave this substitutive and canonic heaven of narratives that are formatted in this way, this superstore of the collectivities, so as to slowly descend towards that singularity bearing, in its secret inner recesses, dark zones in which a personal idiolect emerges from the silent pursuit of existence itself and composes one of its sequences. We are finally returning to the underworld I mentioned earlier. To better enter into the detail of this shadow zone and of the mutations that operate there, this slow descent moves – we have found them again – towards the neighbourhoods where the background noise of hot life transforms its hubbub into monotonous chanting, changes its uproar into psalm, metamorphoses its chaos into musical offering; then, in climbing back up, runs towards layers that are still dark, higher than these neighbourhoods, in which, through an unexplored phase change, this melody, this voice in a nascent state, barely audible, modifies its tumult into articulation, renews its line as *logos*, and does so all the way up to the final stratum, where, always virgin and gleaming with newness, the constitutive language of an inward narrative appears, one whose stuttering beginning, returning over itself as in feedback, relaunches, as a second motor, the initial heat of life itself, feeds it again, augments it in the sense from just now, ties or links it lastly into an original sequence. I still call this emergent language narrative, even though its forms and tonalities have forever abandoned the old temporal and formatted sequence of external events. Like twenty branches and as many heresies, the new narratives bifurcate from these prior formats. I still retain this same word 'narrative' because it preserves the same function, repeated a thousand times, of linking time and life – a life that's less collective, borrowed, public or deceitful, and more faithful, attentive, personal and authentic.

Just as, climbing down the roads of the earth, Orpheus, Homer, Virgil, Jesus Christ or Dante visited ancient underworlds in which old lives vegetated, lives so socially formatted in the past that they became, there, pale shades in dismal meadows of asphodels, so Marcel Proust, quitting, in his turn, these collective formats, descended, by long vertiginous rope-lengths of sentences, towards their original formation, in which time and the soul are found in their nascent state; so James Joyce plunged into the internal and interminable dialogues held by some man or woman in a short day without losing a single word of the brief and indefinite minutes of falling asleep, during which precisely these words emerge; so Franz Kafka penetrated into the labyrinth of a burrow in which a blind animal, terror-stricken, was hiding and dying from anxiety; so, through stylistic techniques, therefore musical with expression, Robert Musil, William Faulkner, Virginia Woolf, Ferdinand Céline . . . opened up as many diverse ways leading to explorations of a time that's living, dreamy or contingently shooting up into a hundred branches, whose percolation, non-linear, transubstantiates, here and there, into a thousand mingled twigs, whose rhythm and tempo infinitely approach the birth of language starting from innermost life and its way, in return, of linking this life.

The tales and histories of the previous literatures often answered the question 'who are we?', but transformed into 'what culture does my life belong to?'; 'what time of a common history must my personal time imitate?'; 'what champion should I choose from this history in order to link my life into a meaningful sequence?';[5] whereas the narratives I just cited celebrate the more recent birth of the individual and his search for identity. Who am I, or, rather, how, in what field, by what linguistic procedures can a, or my, life be brought about by recounting it with the most precision and faithfulness possible? In search of a new world, of a new history, of a humanism lastly, hominescence often quits the old collective formats so as to approach the individual.

[5]History = *histoire*, which, confusingly for a work dealing with narratives and history, can also mean story. I have done my best to discern which sense Serres intends, but I would be remiss if I didn't inform the reader of the possible double meaning the word may have in some passages of this text.

Language and literature

The more literature there is, the more it heads towards the *me*. The more history there is, the more it diverges towards the *we*. The more literature there is, the less history there is, except if thinking is done by means of belongingnesses . . . , and the less redundant engagement and historical approaches to literature there are, yes, the historical approach to literature, that outmoded oxymoron by which societal inflexibility and political tics fail to reach the singular rarity of works. A question whose answer I am seeking remains: What form of narrative will bring us closer to humanity?

In fact, what is literature? As poorly asked here as it was elsewhere for nature or humans, the question transforms. Like me and we and everyone, it is not; it becomes. I can even recount its life: collective in the past, it is becoming more individual; more historical formerly, it is now on the path to singularity. Thus, to return to it, the historical approach to literature applies to archaic narratives, towards which the engaged texts regress. Abandoning essence and being again, I will reformulate the old question: What use do these narratives serve? To construct, starting from life, consciousness and language. The less literature there is, the fewer individuals exist. The fewer free people. We are all today subject to seeking a mask in the megastores of collective mimetism. Literature revitalizes language as much as it does consciousness. What could be more saving? In these times of exacerbated mimetism, literature saves.

Does consciousness forge its first flexions, does it inflect its first folds through this continuous emanation from noise to melody, from melody to tatters of language? I hear my consciousness in the process of forming at the same time as my language forms through this listening. A kind of vortex, a kind of turbulence installs itself, in which, as in feedback, my language maintains the birth of my consciousness and my consciousness maintains the emergence of my language. Said flow of consciousness doesn't flow laminarly but according to this chain of vortices in which the consciousness of oneself and the language of oneself mutually bring each other about. The more and the better I speak, the better and the more I am conscious of myself; the more and the better this consciousness rises to the surface, the better and the more the noises within me cry, chant and end up speaking.

It seems to me that this originary fabrication, which I must have experienced as a child when I didn't yet talk and when I attained the first wails and the recognition of the *ego*, is still going on for me today as a writer of language. The writer ceaselessly returns to these primitive moments, submits his language to the test of the beginning, to the hubbub, then to the harmony in which the *me* itself is created at the same time as this language. For the daily practitioner of sounds, of style, of music, of plaint, of cries and of voice, fairly clumsily blind to the facts or the flow of consciousness, the literary fact is born there, at the same time as me. Consciousness wouldn't exist without language or literature. None of the three would exist without the two others.

You

So the other appears at the same time as me. For my language would remain an idiolect for an autist if a first communication didn't reflect back to me, in sounds, meaning and syntax, an already common language. From the uterus and breast on, my mother must have played this teaching role in the past. As a construction that's continued by style, my maternal language still plays this mirror role, but the men and women who converse with me in a register that's as deep as the one Eurydice dug behind Orpheus's steps permanently play this role again. In the best of cases, every other dialogue constructs external objects or, in the most mediocre cases, the ordeals of a belongingness. You present yourself, of course, at the beginning of this conversation, you who talk to me so often and with such refinement about yourself that I can only deepen myself via this listening. But we will never invent a language from whole cloth that would only belong to ourselves. If we did, we would enclose ourselves, in our turn, in an autism for two. So, at what level are we already plunged in a belongingness, at least a linguistic one, at most a musical one? Starting from the sonorous formation I just said only belonged to me? Everything I just said risks being a lie since, to talk about what happens in my soul, I have ceaselessly appealed to myths, Eurydice, to Orphic musics, to novels, Bovary, to philosophies . . . of a particular culture, mine. Far from inventing or creating, I imitate, cite and repeat. Where should I slide the scalpel which would set to the side what I borrowed from the hypermarket so as to only preserve the authentic? If me and my consciousness are born, with a single voice, at the same time as language, I find myself forced to say that this latter has no need of me in order to be born. So I can only invent a style and can only vary on a given theme.

I quite readily admit that this minuscule margin minimizes the authentic. But if the genetic distance from the bonobo organism to the human, measured by DNA, borders on the minuscule, the distance that separates you, me and a few brothers and sisters from Europe, Asia and Africa diminishes all the way to the impalpable. And yet, in seeing bodies dance, what diversity in charms! We lack an equally precise reference to measure the variations of language, but we are starting to suspect invariants that would even unite linguistic families. Doubtless these distances are due to our ignorances. And yet, in hearing mouths talk or sing, what vast variations! Each author seems a species unto himself alone, each individual a genus and each culture a lineage! The authentic therefore lies in the composition more than in the notes, in the style or the speech more than in the language, in the way the individual is distinguished from the type or the species; it lies less in non-belongingness than in bifurcation in relation to its format. I never invent anything except variations on a given theme. Claiming to only talk about himself and the inventor of a new and dazzling style, what author quotes more than Michel de Montaigne?

We all need a narrative to exist. Need therefore to construct, starting from our noises, an original style that recounts. The originary belongs to the species, the original to the individual. I repeat that I fear, regarding the format, that continuously listening to music across ten technological relays will destroy the inward work of individuation, will cause the consciousness and birth of this inward style to abort in favour of a temporary fashionable community, the way, in the past, epic, tragic . . . literature prevented the personal *ego* from being born in favour of strengthening the political or cultural community, which this literature, truly engaged, extolled. But, as I have also said, language doesn't attack the *ego* as deeply as cries, chants and sonorities, which are anterior to any articulation of meaning. These practices therefore risk destroying the *ego*, the style and the speech of the narrative. Will the forced purchase, the insistency in every place of a conventional music, produce a generation deprived of the attributes the preceding generation thought constructed the human? Will such a generation forget that language, before being used for communication, constructed us as subjects?

But conversely, far from limiting themselves to bringing distances and humans nearer, the new technologies also bring about a new emotive rhythm. When, as a sailor, I wrote to my girlfriend, she received the expressive narrative of my feelings at a moment when, most often, it had vanished from my emotional horizon, fluctuating like the surface of the waters; she collected my soul's past. In return, what could I know of what she was experiencing when I received her missive, on a distant shore, with sometimes an interval of weeks? Following a rhythm with gigantic discontinuities, these epistolary exchanges, another literary genre, couldn't link the times of her life nor the times of my own, still less the language whose tatters were attempting to recite our relations.

Now equipped with email or mobile phones, we can both talk or write to each other at the precise moment when some emotion assails us, when that decision seems to impose itself upon us . . ., messages whose contents, received in real time by the correspondent, at the instant when she decides or is moved in her turn, link, without any discontinuity, the disparate words and instants of our two lives, united by love, and therefore weave their relation by means of this narrative that is never truly interrupted, traversed with traps and sometimes misunderstandings, but reinvented in real time. In comparison to the maritime rhythms from just now, quite similar to those that Ulysses, singing in Alcinous's palace, only maintained in silence with Penelope, remaining in Ithaca in the midst of the suitors, it's no longer a matter of the same space, obviously, nor of the same rhythms and *tempi*, nor of the same sounds, nor of the same emotion, nor of the same sharing, nor of the same continuum of style, nor of the same narrative, nor therefore of the same loves, nor of the same souls, nor maybe of the same bodies . . . In another time and in other words, another *I* has just been born, supported by a new other.

The new technologies don't only transform the aforementioned cognitive faculties, memory and imagination, formerly subjective and today objectivized, as *Hominescence* and *Branches* described in detail, but also the secret zones of innermost emotivity at the very sources of having one's own style, in short, the decisively human depths of the *psyche.* I mean by these words the sites previously described in which elementary life becomes speech and style in us, an inchoative discourse that, in return, changes life into and links it as destiny. Shared in this way, the emotive unites with the cognitive to change the human.

Two levels tier my emotive soul. When speech is born, it immediately seems to know how to distinguish, from among the affects, passions and feelings . . . into clear and, so to speak, classifiable species: I find myself motivated by envy, overwhelmed by fear, shaking with jealousy, swollen with anger, traversed by hatred. . . . But, before or below, when speech, in its nascent state, is still stammering and muddled up, these species appear melted into prior genuses, a little like the way a trunk precedes its branches. Limpid and distinct, speech readily judges this primitive magma to be confused, but music, before speech, expresses its mixture with exactitude because it knows how to sing the universals of affect before words isolate them into differentiated feelings. Better: music causes our universals to be heard before articulated meaning appears. The rhythms and notes are immersed in a genus whose species are analyzed by letters and sentences.

Eminently endowed for language, you, woman, drag about wonderfully a sunny landscape in which a hundred singular emotions, discernible and variable, are distributed into copses, high forests, cliffs and hills, river mouths and shores, an entire Map of Tender that you equally see, entirely unfurled, around the speech of the person talking to you. Thus, you are judged to be intuitive, while they should say instead that your genius is discursive. A blanket of fog, on the contrary, conceals from the male, me for instance, awake only at sunset, the borders between the fields and the forest, between the differential species of emotion; instead of a Map of Tender, my gaze only disposes of a sea route chart, representing oceans for an intercontinental navigation; almost empty, this portolan chart only lets appear, right in the middle of absent shores, two or three islands, never the swell's local wrinkles. You know how to ice skate, without catching an edge, on a frozen lake, amid the multiple drawings of a hardened frost; under fog signals, I sail and navigate, blind, on wide vague waves. The cognitive of our affective realms differs like words and sounds, speech and music; we find ourselves strangers here, not like diverse species, but exactly like genus and species, the muddled rough-draft man remaining upstream from the neat final-copy female. The one, branch; the other, twig. The soul starts with the male and develops into woman, the way

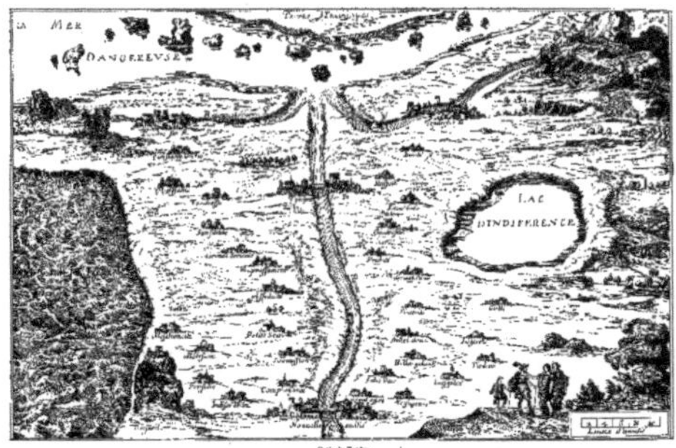

Figure 1 *Clélie*'s Map of Tender. Vintage book illustration from Larousse du XXème siècle 1932. Public domain.

speech is born from music before ripening into words and verbs. In these matters, my weakness comes from the fact that, as a male by flesh and soul, I never knew how to speak or write, while I have dreamed of composing songs and cantatas my entire life long. Ideas come to me in sounds. As a writer, I judge myself to be a failed musician. Thus, do I know what I experience except via masses in fusion?

Spaces

So let's compare a few maps. Even though I'm a sailor, as I said, I never tire of wandering on the Map of Tender, a world map of love. The soul stretches out, unfolds and fluctuates in a space in which our language claims to describe the soul by taking its measurements: longanimous, magnanimous, pusillanimous; long or big or greedy, appallingly mediocre. I don't know the properties of such an expanse, but I am moved by contemplating the way, with an entirely feminine distinction, Scudéry's *Clélie* describes it. In the land of Tender, inclination flows like a river, indifference remains stable in a lake, hatred rages with the sea, pride [*orgueil*] perches on a rock. Great Heart [*Grand Coeur*] and Sincerity live in two villages, and cities are built on the riverbanks of Esteem and Recognisance. From Tenderness [*Tendresse*] to Assiduity, we visit our amorous relation the way we would stroll in a land we chose to frequent together and into which we ventured with or without reliability in orientation, since somewhat unpleasant paths can lead us from Attentiveness [*Empressement*] to Submission or from Indiscretion to the Sea of Enmity [*Mer d'Inimité*]. Let's rest in Probity before yielding to Forgetfulness [*Oubli*]. The soul lets a polite landscape be seen.

On a dark and entirely masculine night, Saint John of the Cross ascended towards Carmel, across lane and trail, towards a roadless mountain where springs shot up amid the offered fruits. The mystic route chart describes vague genuses instead of clear species.

Freud borrowed from Maxwell, the physicist, and from Listing, the topologist, the spatial schema of the complex: for the electricians of the era used this name, so common today that we have forgotten its origin, for a lattice assembly grouping together resistances and capacitances, in short, wires and plates permitting energy transfers . . ., a multiple and highly sophisticated apparatus, at the far poles of which the potential difference is nullified. In a global network in which this complicated assembly would intervene locally, everything happens as though this assembly didn't exist since no difference, at its limits, would cause it to be noticed. Whether it is connected or not to the general network changes nothing in its total behaviour. It exists, of course, and even powerfully from the internal and local point of view of the interlaced nodes and paths, of the transfers and forces that are exchanged there, but it becomes annihilated, completely nullified in the general fabric. Even if the landscape, even if the map is reduced here to constructed circuits, as on an air route chart, this is the original spatial model of the unconscious! Effective nonetheless, a space is nullified here.

Who can contest the precision of such movements across such places, in the land of Tender or the Mount of Mysticism as well as in the unconscious apparatus? I defy anybody to describe the arcana of the *psyche* without yielding to the intuition of some expanse in which motions, transfers and transformations would take place. Bergson, who wanted our intelligence, devoted to space, to never be able to attain the pure temporal flow, reserved for consciousness, didn't win his battle because he confused his space with Euclid's space and likened it to metrics. But we now conceive of expanses of all types, including qualitative ones without any measurement; consequently, Bergsonian duration still flows in a space, like a river and its turbulence. The soul remains spatiotemporal. We are enhancing its relief.

Internal or external?

So let's acknowledge the necessity of a landscaped expanse in psychology. What area does introspection pass through? In what site are my emotions triggered? Where are my feelings heading? Above what threshold do they change? Where do they gush up from? These common questions of site seem, even here, relevant. In other words, from what unfolded exteriority is the inward woven?

How does it happen that your sadness, audible, tangible, sayable, colours the skies today with yellow or that my joy, musical and white, fills, generous, warm and blessed, the air I breathe all the way to the horizon? If the gushing up of emotion makes sensibilities that enchant the landscape come out of me, conversely, the surrounding landscape paints inward space and has an effect on it. When I was ploughing the furrows at the arse-end of my two oxen, I didn't recite my life to myself in the same way as when, in front of my computer, I remembered, so as to describe it, that scene from my youth; effort, heat and bad weather exist in the first case, hard and material-based; there is nothing but the soft in the other one, purely logos-based. The person who sweats doesn't endure the same soul or doesn't enjoy it in the same way as the person who believes he thinks. When the sun sets over Garonne, it doesn't show its green ray the way it does on the Red Sea, nor the mirages that make one believe that the desert cliffs have suddenly transformed into a metropolis bristling with skyscrapers. Here, there's no risk of me lapsing into magic; there, my soul believes in miracles. Here, the *Discourse on the Method*; there, the *One Thousand and One Nights*. When, at the crack of dawn, it tackles, with a piolet, an ice couloir illuminated with a deep purple translucency, *lumen de lumine*, what soul, surrounding the alpinist's body, wouldn't lapse into the sacred?

The landscape acts on me through labour, easy or demanding; food, abundant or rare; the climate, wet or dry; its inhabitability, through its smiling horizons or its arid austerity. I depend on it for my life and its length, for my body and its comforts, for my soul and its ardours; I depend on it for my mood. As much as it likes and without wanting to, my soul becomes desert-like, solar, icy, leafy, bovine, winged, serpentine, sounding with gloomy winds or bird music. Surrounded by insects and venomous snakes, marsupials and wild camels, does my Aboriginal friend from the Australian Outback, a nomad dragging behind himself sixty thousand years without agriculture or livestock breeding due to the absence of mammals and grasses in his ancestral desert, have the same *self* as his contemporary, a doctor in Melbourne, living in a seaside villa, adept at sailboarding and fed with bovine meat since the Neolithic? My narrative enters into my landscape, and the landscape acts in my narrative. To take up again the abandoned question 'who am I?', here is my answer: the bushiness of my narrative amid the leafiness of my landscapes, external and inward.

We already knew that the body has the shape of a torus, that the space of the mouth, throat, oesophagus, pylorus and intestine all the way to the anus . . . remains, its entire length, on the outside, in such a way that our organism turns around this emptiness, sometimes occupied with what we put there. This reasoning is surprising, so much do we consider our own viscera to be, literally, intestine or inward; yet I would like to repeat this reasoning for blood circulation and other things, leading to other orifices. Let's air out the body, more outside itself, more given over to outside space than we had believed. Likewise, I compare the soul to that three-dimensional variety of a Möbius strip called a Klein bottle, for which no one can decide what lies outside or inside: where are the Tender, Mount Carmel, the complex located? Do we in fact understand what we are saying when our speech expresses the inward? So tell me where speech comes from? From the mouth, the lungs? Which are external. What are you talking about? Your complexes?

Onto landscapes I dream about and don't know how to situate, Tender or Carmel, onto those I have inhabited or that my travels have externally crossed, how can I not overprint those of my readings and my imagination? I have sailed on ten Atlases, in colour and on paper, even longer than on the real oceans; in the company of Captain Nemo, I have observed, from his living room, through the Nautilus's porthole, a thousand underwater species cited in printed textbooks; Cousteau's images have taken me on board the *Calypso*, but as well, one of Ulysses's companions, I have wandered on the smile of the divine sea, beneath the rosy-fingered dawn; I have been shipwrecked as he has; alas, Nausicaa, playing ball with her companions on the sand, has rarely saved me from the waters and agreed to pull the miserable seaweed hanging on my flesh off me. My inward tapestry is printed with a thousand global maps of paper or of dreams.

Beneath these piled-up maps lie, even more active although dormant and subterranean, like tectonic plates, the primal waters of the hubbub, preparing the musical stasis, the hundred-fruited Eden, my paradise, the well of marriage engagements from which the patriarchs drank, my thirsts for women, the Mount Sinai of my ecstasies, the Exodus desert, Job's misery, the black desperation of my days of sorrow, my carnal and mystical love affairs in the Song of Songs and the love affairs of my Queens of Sheba, the Sea of Galilee and its miraculous fishing, where I thought I was on Garonne with her schools of shad that covered the waters, plethoric moments of superabundance, the summit of the Transfiguration and of my transports, the Mount of Olives, Golgotha, my torments, the road to Emmaus, my encounters . . . I am walking along in the dust of the footpaths of Palestine, not knowing whether they travel the rocky dryness between Jerusalem and Jericho or through my internal land. I wasn't born there; none of my ancestors fished or looked after herds there; I only spent a few weeks there, but, in a way, I recognize my land there, the place where the One was born who, on one night of desperate joy, stole from me the inwardness of my inwardness. Who am I? Who knows? But where am I? Look at the Alpine mountain around the Col de la Bonette; you alone know that, if you contemplate it, you will see my soul. Who can situate it, outside or inside?

Ego sive natura

We all need a narrative to exist. We create ourselves. The author *I* stands both outside and inside the actor *I*.

The biblical narrative drew dazzling consequences from the emergence of a language so incredibly human that it became divine because of this. The omniscient author of the text, the all-powerful author of the things of the world and of the history of people, created the world with that speech experts call performative. God said *fiat*, and it happened. Author and creator merged. The human authors of a thousand subsequent narratives knew that they never create anything but text, signs on paper, shadows on a screen. Except, precisely, for authors of autobiographies, who, for their part, know that the language of the *I* creates the *I*, as performative as the speech of God producing the things of the world. Each of us, through our style, becomes his own creator. Before judging Jean-Jacques, Rousseau created him. I exist by means of the narrative I tell myself or write. *Ego sive Deus*.

We are beginning to know how to read, decode, translate and decipher a hundred new languages outside of the ones we speak: the language of crystals, of stellar colours, the language of radioactivity, of biochemistry . . . don't depend on our projects. We have just discovered an extensive set of non-human languages. Written, the world knows how to write. The lights of the sky trace the gnomon's shadow lines on the sundial's plate; across the plain, the streaming waters engrave the gentle curves of the river basin; erosion sculpts the mountain; rocks store the moment of their cooling; strata pile up like paragraphs, landscapes pass like pages, cliffs seem volumes; the dusts from the atmosphere mark the age of their descent on ice cores; radioactive elements count out their age; across the Universe, the Big Bang traced the cosmic microwave background forever; DNA programmes part of the individual to come and launches translation machines in him; the genetic code, for its part as well, has a performative power; it dictates, and it happens. Does a landscape or some shore, fractal, exist on which one can't, in the end, read a thousand lines; a sound emanating in the air, the ground or the water that one can't, in the end, hear; and in both cases understand like words?

As many languages explode into writings, themselves diversified into as many written forms as there are states of things. Whether inanimate or living, the universe speaks like us, writes like us, tells and expresses itself like us, creates data banks, remembers, translates and even sometimes, mutating, errs or lies, but rarely. This Ptolemaic revolution of language decenters it from us.[6] Will objective languages surpass human idioms in number? Does nature remove us from our linguistic exclusivity? Who, today, expected this new revolution, wounding, once again, human narcissism?

Talking about themselves, writing about and on themselves, do the things of the world tell, performatively, for their part as well, their autobiographies? Yes. The Universe, the Earth and life know how to recount their origin, tell their evolution, relate the contingent bifurcations of their time, and sometimes let the era of their disappearance be glimpsed. A vast narrative issues from the world. Do the things themselves know themselves? Perhaps. Can we conceive of a self-knowing on the part of the world?

Am I bound to find narratives or confessions in the inanimate and the living? Thus, when I am writing my own confessions, am I aware that, as a fractal fragment of the universe, I am imitating galaxies, the planet, the crowd of molecules, radioactive particles, the deer's belling or the peacock's plumage, vaingloriously unfurled? Thus, the little story that creates me enters into the Grand Narrative of the world as a part. I tell myself and know myself the way nature tells itself and knows itself. The most inwardly secret inside unites with the most colossally unfurled outside. Before starting this book, did I know that she or he who recounts herself or himself comes closest to things? The speaking subject mixes his noise with the noise of the resonant objects. I write like light, crystals or streams; I recount myself like the world.

I am beginning to hear the languages of humans and the languages of things at the same time; I am thinking of the bridge that would unite them. Deafened, dazzled, I am discovering the universality of language and of the written, their global saliency in

---

[6]Serres most likely sees this Ptolemaic revolution as the opposite of Kant's Copernican revolution, for which objects are determined by the mind.

the subjective and the affective, the cognitive and the objective. I hear the panlinguistic vibration emitted by the cables of this performative bridge that links me to others, to God and to the world: *ego sive homo sive Deus sive natura*.

Existing in truth, lying in order to exist

If God, omniscient and truthful, doesn't err, they say, or lie, if nature itself doesn't deceive, can I, myself, call myself veridical and infallible? No. Of course, I can be mistaken regarding some factual point; of course, my narrative can lie, but, in unifying scattered elements, it says something else, something less of the order of truth than of the order of existence. It puts me in the world. We all need a narrative to subsist. In saying this, I vibrate between false and true at least as much as I did just now between external and inward, subjective and natural. Do I exist at the high price of truth? I don't know, but I do know, in any case, that a game is being played here that, surpassing the game of the authentic and the falsifiable, has as its stakes life and death. I would vanish from not telling myself. So the narrative matters to me so much that I have to weave it at all costs for the thread of my time to continue. Existence is at stake. By spinning the text of my story, I am weaving the thread of my life, the way the Fates did. Should I no longer have anything to tell or recount, I must quickly invent so as to fill this hole of nothingness whose emptiness I often feel and live. So, panic-stricken, I augment. I exaggerate, swell up, replace. I create or I lie? At the ethical risk of lying, at the emotional risk of paranoia, I take myself to be a creator god having performative speech: I believe, whether firmly convinced or in bad faith, that I am truly living the way I say I am and desperately try to make it be believed. Becoming a false and deceitful god, I exchange the truth for my life; I lie in order to exist. Does pathology, which finds me to be sick, or morality, which judges me to be deceitful, take into account this augmentation, which comes from the panic of dying without this swelling, this oedema or this life preserver fluctuating on the sea of Nothing?

The word 'author' has, as I have said, its origin in this verb 'augment'. Where does this widening, this exaggerating pomposity come to it from? Speech rounds the cheeks, pushes the lips forward, blows wind, influences souls. So do I talk loudly and high and mighty? Whatever I may say, my sonorous words exceed silent facts; my language shifts away from mute events. Narrative doesn't create the *I* that lives and acts in reality, exactly. Between saying, soft, and doing, hard, an energy or information shift persists at least. As a result, the stake and the anxiety of existing, for real and true, surpasses the concern for truthful authenticity. I even toy with the idea that if I always confined myself to strict faithfulness, by implacably planing down the imaginary, the compassionate, the logic of fuzzy sets, the blind hope of projects, the mad anxiety of enduring, in brief, the virtual, the unreal, the possible and dream, I would enter into a psychological rigidity of such a sharp rigour that it would prevent me from living and would forbid those around me their comforts.

So I sometimes pay less attention to the veracity of what is being said than to its aura, its possible radiance, the enthusiasm it communicates and the warmth it spreads; this is why, sailing on the long waves of the voice, I speak better than I write. Eloquence lifts the flesh the way a penny's worth of yeast aerates the dough. The raw, clear and precise truth often seems flat, mechanical, cruel and aseptic to me. A man of the theatre, perhaps, a novelist, a storyteller in any case, I didn't have to quit childhood fascinations with coming-of-age journeys. I believe that, enchanting, language is valuable due to its musical bases, its rhythm, forms and colours, and that it came about for us so that we can live, dance and take flight, so that, due to its sounds, we can construct another world, our own – light – one. As an extravagant example, the translucent truths of mathematics fascinate me less due to their demonstrative rigour than by building a thousand ice palaces whose architectural structures full of inexhaustible wonders I never tire of visiting; in this paradise, an unbelievable accumulation of evident facts twists good sense's intuition so often and attains discoveries that are so torturous that the truth there acquires the transcendent status of ecstasy; I learned there to love the true under the aforementioned conditions of enchantment. As for inward truths, they are accompanied in me by such an unfurling of emotions – consequently, I see emotions more than states; therefore, movement better than stable things – that I perceive them to be trembling, less with blurriness and obscurity than with an excessive light; I see them poorly through excess rather than lack. The enthusiastic fox: this old totem, my genuine name given to me in my adolescence so accurately, uncovers inside me this brilliant divinity or this burning demon who have never unclenched their claws or stopped their benedictions and whose double presence has continually produced there a state of getting carried away, periphery harmonics, an exaggerated augmentation of things and events such that, heard from outside, they can seem to lapse into falsity and lie, even into mask, whereas I undergo and express them as highlighting, as accentuation of a voice, of a joy, of a despair that seek to have themselves heard from afar or from far below, or better, that seek to guide the interlocutor in the direction of that other world I have never stopped hoping for. I have never jumped, spoken, thought, run, loved, walked, danced, swum, laughed or cried except as propelled by hope.

I always hope, today and every minute, for something other than what I see, another world than this one, revolting with violence and ugliness, another human than the one I believe myself to be; shifted by hope, I live this alterity, between these two branches. In the other person, I make out a hero, a genius, a saint or the goddess of my days; a haloed lamp, no, I don't see clearly, I see floodlit. So why do you think I live between the lines of books or narratives? For better and worse, this excessive and oblique light blinds and impassions me, tortures and enchants me. I feel the internal third party that is enthusiasm inside me like the devil and the Good Lord. It saves me and damns me. It allows me to survive. I live, love and think not so much with my two feet planted on the incontestable earth of the evident truth as distraught and lost, tossed between hell and heaven.

Descartes presented intuition and deduction as two operations of the mind. They in fact characterize two varieties of mind that suffer from the fear of not experiencing their pleasure; the one ritualizes the route so as to attain this; the other nullifies the route by chasing without mediation. The first one constructs a method, a logic, opens up a route cadenced with milestones and resting places; the other one claims that no path already opened up allows finding the new. The one, active, deductive, inductive, a seducer, chases after women; the other one waits for them in its bed. This latter demonstrates and goes to the true; the former recounts and can be mistaken. Slow, the one evokes the clarity of things and the sureness of reason; fast, the other one hears and sees, launches into the immediate, invokes chaos theory, takes bifurcations and hops here and there. I side rather with this one.

Death and rebirth

We all need a narrative to exist. The narrative of a straight method rarely errs; intuition stumbles upon the truth by often being mistaken. Vibrating, at least twice, between false and true as between the external and the inward, the subjective and the objective, my narrative of emotional joy also vibrates between nothingness and existence. Without narrative, I am worth nothing. Beyond error and truth, I am nothing, ontologically speaking. Like Ulysses the sailor, my name is Nobody. Captain Nemo commands a submarine that no one has ever seen, plunged into the deepest of seas; an inward black box vanishes in an external black box. The call – *Michel!* – covers over these two emptinesses. Behind this exclamation sound, nobody truly responds. The difficulty I experience descending into the innermost recesses of internal consciousness doesn't only come from the fact that I don't see them, but, perhaps, from the fact that they do not exist. Who am I? This black box. Dark, stripped of specifications; or, on the contrary, white, equivalent to anything at all. To get myself out of this hell, out of this fundamental nothingness, out of this black, out of this translucent white, both of them empty, I invent my life, plan it, construct it, shape it, represent it to myself, recount it. We need a tremendous talent to falsify our nothingness in this way. I admire the genius, properly divine, of those humans who, before us, invented the individual. It took at least a god to pull us from this nothing, from this nothingness, from the emptiness I experience inside me all the time in the most real way possible. Does narrative thus create the *self* starting from nothingness the way God creates the world *ex nihilo*, starting from nothing? Might this miracle, which you doubt for the external world, become a daily act in the inward world?

How can the narrative I have been conducting for several pages, poorly stitched together, tattered with borrowings, inventions, confessions, memories, attentions and oversights, exits and plungings, unify my life? Time rarely flows linearly; most often it percolates, as I have often said. The inventions of consciousness, of speech and of narrative, those autopoieses, cross percolation thresholds, as though scattered parts were linked together in successive levels. Successful or strung together, how do these linkings function?

Not only was I born and am I going to die, but my representable time runs from here to there, where I remain stable across transformations. Above, identity designated both the logical principle $A \equiv A$ and the principle of individuation $I \equiv I$; it indicates both nomination and stability, the same and myself, *idem* and *ipse*.

My name is Michel and, from birth to death throes, I remain fairly similar to this Michel, even under twenty avatars, foreign to one another: mason, peasant, sailor, writer. So, and thirdly, are there two additional identities: the me, identical and named, who lives and acts in silence or talks to others absent-mindedly, and the me who recounts myself? How are we to distinguish actor from author? Does the one who acts merge with the one who relates the narrative? No doubt there is a gap between the second one and the first, even in autobiography, in which the one who lives represents, in real time, his life to himself. Were we to remain plunged, immersed, in temporal, vital and worldly immanence, the narrative wouldn't be able to be said, constituted, gathered together, unified; it would lose consistency and duration, like the unity of its subject. The gap between the actor and the author allows this latter to glimpse a quasi-totality, to perceive the actor in his performances, to stabilize his identity across his adventures and avatars. By means of his speech, the author detaches himself from the immanence in which the actor plunges, swims and struggles. By means of this doubling, by means of this distance between two presences, by means of this outlet hole that is representation, the warp and woof of the narrative is woven; by means of this fold or this hole, the cement of my life flows and hardens. This gap in time, in the nothingness, in the subject, in existence, this distance that tends to overflow projects, dreams and their rare fulfillments, the beginning and the end, birth and death, lets another dimension emerge, transcendence.

Located in the Underworld in times past, outside the world, outside history, outside the acts of bodies and of souls, the Fates spun, wove and then broke the threads of lives. I have to, like them, put myself outside of my life in order to compose a text of it. Without this new outside, no one would be able to link together a narrative; pure immanence would come undone into disjointed scraps, told by an idiot, full of sound and fury. This other dimension conditions the narrative. This outlet hole that is transcendence, where the three Fates bustle, keeps death at a distance. How are we to move away from death, talk about it, how are we to represent it to ourselves, without placing ourselves not before it, an entirely commonplace view, one hiding the genuine end, but above all after it? How are we to live a life without imagining its end? How are we to live our lives without suffering death?

In the *Odyssey*, the *Aeneid*, the Gospels, the *Divine Comedy* . . ., a descent into the Underworld, once again, conditions narrative; there isn't one narrative that doesn't pierce through the black barrier; there is no major work that doesn't bear this shadowy hole . . ., a dark doorway by which I finally see my time summed up; there is no narrative without its end as a stop, without its end as a goal, without its end announced, experienced along its duration, without the intense suffering of this term, without this pain that sometimes causes my throat and my time to choke up, that forces me to reinvent myself minute by minute like a continuous creation, that compels me, because I carry it in real time, to patiently recount it to myself. By this fissure that's bleeding and weeping with passion and patience, you will recognize a life become a narrative, which can become a work, you will recognize a work.

There can be no successful life without this fissure of a failed life, without an accursed share of defeats and pains, those little differential deaths, without fire burning the ramparts or shipwreck on the open sea, desert crossings, exile, exodus, without slavery or captivity, falling into poverty and dereliction, without abandonment, anguish or exclusion, without birth in the straw, passion or crucifixion. Why? Because we cannot see our lives without the shift opened up by the proximity of death, without experiencing its pain. My present is represented after my death. As in one's final throes, life struggles against death.

Experiencing, in the wrenching, this gap of transcendence allows us to see immanence in its totality, to represent it to ourselves, to describe it, to lament it, to sing it, in brief, to recount it. Without this mortal wound, we would remain plunged in the oceanic plane of immanence without perceiving higher, with each stroke, than the crest of the waves, the luck of the breeze or the currents of contingency. He who plays at holing himself up in the plane of immanence obviously forgets the space in which this plane is plunged and without which no one could construct or conceive it; whatever the finitude he may lament, he can only think this island amid the sea, on which the one who laments sails and from which he sees it; he only knows its topography on the basis of a space he inhabits and from which he draws up a map of it.

There can be no narrative, and probably no abstraction, without such a transcendence, and no transcendence without experience of the seven sorrows. No memoirs without beyond the tomb. The transformation of a life into narrative passes through this experience of death, through this vertiginous gap, through the fall into Avernus, through the resurrection. All narrative suscitates life, resuscitates or resurrects survival. The genius of Christianity launched a narrative that puts a failed life forward as an example of a successful life, a failed life begun in cow dung, continued in a wandering without home or table and ending with a murderous execution. A minuscule existence crowned, after death, by resurrection. Likewise, accompanied by the passion of death, the narrative of my little life resurrects me. Tears of joy.

WE

COLLECTIVE NARRATIVES

Death, again

Revolted by the Hiroshima flash, as an adolescent, I reviewed my pitiless culture; I remember chewing over our history crushed with weapons, courage, blood and tears. Its movement – preserved by written transmission, the pride of our culture – began with endless wars under the walls of Troy or Jericho, with inevitable battles dominated by admirable figures, Achilles or Samson, wielding sabres or jawbones of an ass. Under the permanent regime of perpetual conflicts, its narrative never ceased to anaesthetize our sensibilities sufficiently to make us envy the fate of those who kill or die, as though death by collective sacrifice had become the ultimate goal and meaning of the time of our lives and of our memories.

Xenophon spilled Persian blood; Jephthah the blood of the children of Ammon; Livy murdered Albans, Sabines, Etruscans and Carthaginians; Julius Caesar exterminated Gauls; Roland the braggart made us believe that he only carved in rock; Saint Louis won his saintliness by combatting the Arab and eradicating the Cathars; Shakespeare's kings, El Cid, the Horatii, the soldiers of the French Revolutionary Army, the victims of the guillotine, the Napoleon legend, continually revivified, mortified rather, by colonial conquests and two world wars, fired up our youth to the point of making us believe that it was necessary to give our lives and to take the lives of brothers we were persuaded to hate from the other side of the borders and seas so that our fathers, teaching a base morality of resentment, courage and heroism, might kill their sons without any risk.[1]

Today still, as on that morning, I see my culture and my history as an abominable river whose overflowing abundance sweeps along blood and scattered limbs, beneath the cries of crows and the sobbing of women, white widows of combatants who died in the prime of their lives, a mowed-down sex.

That towards which a movement blindly rushes, its end, sometimes expresses the movement clearly. It didn't have any goal, of course, but should it finally reach some place, interpreted then as a target, this attainment will reveal its past. As with the future perfect, one imagines one reads its complete destination as the intention of its impetus.

Suddenly widened, stopped, motionless, fixed, this historical flow then began to rot. Over the entire world, the unbreathable pestilential odour of Western history spread. I have felt it, lived it, understood it: Alexander, the young conqueror, decomposes into Hitler; crowned with laurels, Julius Caesar putrefies into Mussolini; Napoleon rots into Stalin and Marshal Foch into Pol Pot; the hoplites, the Crusaders, the Grenadiers of the Guard, all those who departed carrying their rifles with innocent enthusiasm . . . , here they are again, corrupted into Nazis, infected into Stalinians, spoiled into kamikazes, gangrened into fundamentalists, mouldered into those who wield the axe of the Good. The ancient heroes are revealed in the uncovered faces of contemporary murderers.

The illustrious figures of our culture reappeared in their true and faithful light thanks to the reeking truth of our twentieth century and its tens of millions of corpses, a century whose genius in one fell swoop recapitulated, by maximizing them all the way to their zenith, every abomination gradually perpetrated over the time that

[1] 'Mortified' is to be understood in its etymological sense of to put to death.

had preceded, a century that struck the final symphonic chord of the little prior polyphonies, a century that settled the entire debt our fathers only paid off in small change. A victim of historical indigestion, our time vomited up its past by giving its summary, its addition, its synthesis, its integral and by expressing clearly the meaning of every historical and cultural horror we were forced to swallow, imitate and admire. So I knew that, from afar or from anear, Stalin, already, was being prepared in Napoleon, Hitler in Alexander and Mussolini in Julius Caesar; the rough draft Foch preceded the final draft Pol Pot; the sketch that was the eradicated Gauls and Cathars readied the working drawing that became the Shoah; an ancient rough outline, the capture of Troy opened up the actuality of the bombing of Dresden. One after the other, distant or near, all these figures promised the fulfilment, the completion of their project. These hurried attempts ran towards their Truth, unveiled from then on. Our cultures teach murder. I read the meaning of history in the blood and the goal of history in the crimes against humanity. And since this truth is finally appearing on a giant screen, the hope that sounds, finally, the end of this era is rustling.

This fulfilment of the promises my history gives a thousand scattered images of, this precisely is the revelation that the twentieth century brought. With a vast hope, I call the entire epoch inhuman that preceded it and which it ended because this word 'epoch' signifies, of course, the duration of an era, but, more profoundly, more literally, in a more decisive manner, indicates that a segment, begun here, finished there; that a parenthesis, opened with writing in a distant time, was closed on that date; that what began beneath the Trojan walls and was perpetuated from cannons to cuirasses and from torpedoes to bombs, from generation to generation, had its finishing touches put on it in the heights of horror of my childhood; that, slowly raised, caressed, prepared, matured, educated, instructed, pampered, illustrated, delicately bedecked with flowers, deafeningly sung of . . . over several thousand years of murderous culture, the thanatological Beast revealed itself, total, in the clouds of Hiroshima. Not so much the swan song as the final howl of the Leviathan History. On this path of culture, let's hope that we shall not go farther than this revelation. So this epoch has closed.

The libido of belongingness

We participated in the belongingness illustrated by such bloody heroes. We had to battle the Trojans, Persians, Philistines, barbarians, *those ferocious soldiers* who spoke different languages, who inhabited the other side of the mountains, who ate, drank, loved and governed themselves differently and belonged to different groups.[2] Our heroes make our history, which makes our heroes, who together make our subset. Who are we? Participants in our belongingness.

No doubt we cannot do without it. We love in couples, eat in families, live in our region, collaborate in the affairs of cities or professions, think according to our corporatisms, speak our patois, care about our cultures and sometimes our countries, the whole of it in company with associates, proud of a common civilization. But this passion, whose intensity enchants our happiness and binds us to those close to us, to peers, to fellows, also leads to violence. Disputes between tribes, wars of nations, class struggles: rivalry, as much and more than persons, sets the groups we enjoy being part of into opposition. Did the deluge of fire and blood in which my childhood was bathed stream with this heavy libido of belongingness, dense with sound and fury, with inexpiable murders, with imprescriptible culpabilities? I have suspected this my entire life. But can we dream of living without community? Must, here too, love be mixed with hatred and solidarity with sacrificial murder?

No doubt we cannot do without belongingness. Here we are on the wall, the guide, my female friend and me. Discreet joy.

---

[2]The phrase in italics is from 'La Marseillaise'.

In our roped team, which has already been formed for a long time now, each of us knows how the other will react and even anticipates his or her behaviour. A word, a cry, a discreet call, a trembling of the rope suffices to communicate the indispensable detail. Economical, intentions respond to gestures and silences to muteness. The roped team grips and caresses the mountain, which responds, mute, to the team. The rope writes its line on the route already traced on the wall. We only chat away during the walk on the approach, in dialogues having free hands and elbow room. Hands and feet tied by the transcendent presence of the mountain, our bodies and souls become transparent. We will speak freely once again on the summit, when untied. Between the base and the summit, tacit agreements about detail, a silent contract about the whole. Who climbs the route? Not you, not me, not him or her: *we*. But what to call this *we* of the roped party? How to say or describe what happens without words? *We*: tight-knit, tied together; *we*: under the contract of the rope. Do you want to see, touch and experience the social contract in the most vivifying concreteness? Come climbing with us in Pelvoux, and you will observe the role of the rope. It unites us, we who are in love, passionate about beauty, we who are juridical and religious. The light joy of acting together.

Horror. Fed from childhood with inexpiable wars, a contemporary of tens of millions of deaths, forever nauseated with corpses, I have long vomited up the ideologies of assemblage that, accentuating the status of countries, parties, sects or classes, impelled their militants, militaries, citizens, sectarians and committed individuals of every stripe to die, bleeding, for the corresponding Leviathan. I flee the raging mob and its cries of fury; I hate pressure groups, allied to conquer power and spread, while disguising it, injustice. Upon hearing sociology defined as a combat sport, I quickly became a pacifist. I preferred small teams, quickly dissolved, our climbing party in the high mountains, my old light boats, cooperatives, the sporting associations drifting towards folklore. I have consequently spent my time, often with regret, on solitary labours, while, nonetheless, I love community life, whether one of science or exercise, enjoy sharing labour, work, bread, wit, laughter and parties, playing with and for others. Like the tongue for Aesop and the passion love, the collective leads us to crime and happiness, to the worst and the best. Necessary and dangerous.

The crisis of the collective

A question: Speaking honestly, what collective, today, do my contemporaries and I really have any desire to become members of? Supposing a certain libido of belongingness entices us, to what address should we bring adherence, signature and enthusiasm, to the point of consecrating all or part of our days to it? Individualism, which my learned contemporaries sometimes complain about, was also born from this disgust over murders perpetrated by the ideologies that destroyed my youth, spent walking alongside the dead in ditches. Cite the collective worthy enough for consent, belief, acts, even existential commitment to be invested in it. A kind of sceptical relativism distances us from this choice. How many institutions that unleashed the enthusiasm of our parents now resemble those stars whose light is received by our eyes but which science shows to have died ages ago? Their coldness doesn't attract many people any more.

Beyond a possible choice, the question instead revolves around the intensity of the investment required. We need to live in a group; I admit this at the same time as my friends. We have just enlisted in this one. What energy does it require? Do we have to live and die for it? The answer shoots forth: no. What group today merits the sacrifice of our lives? The country? I have already given it the soul of my youth. I don't willingly recite or sing the calls to murder of 'La Marseillaise'. And I invite my fellows to forget the noisy words of that hymn, even if rulers, stemming from another age, would like our children to learn to suck its blood by heart. Because those others, who come from elsewhere and are participants in another group, can no longer be considered today, without committing a crime against humanity, as enemies, as 'ferocious soldiers who are coming right into our arms to cut the throats of our sons and our women'. No, we will no longer give our lives nor offer those of our descendants to murder these neighbours, at least European ones, or at most human ones. In front of my students, faced with my successors, I will instead call them brothers by adoption and will invite them to come, right into my arms, to laugh and dine with my woman and – why not? – court my daughters and great-nieces. Up until my death, and through adoptive dilection, I will sing of human filiation rather than this hatred. If being a member of my country demands this ignominy, I might as well withdraw into individualism. No enthusiasm inflames me for these howls of aggression. I no longer want to believe in this narrative nor sing this base racism of an 'impure blood'. No one any longer, at least in France and the West, at most in the world, can listen to such harangues. Nothing could be worse than only loving those within one's group. No group, simply human, justifies investing one's life, except perhaps, precisely, the supernatural, which is superhuman, or global humanitarian projects; in every one of these instances, nothing authorizes spilling the blood of others.

Without saying so, governments know this since soldiering is becoming a profession again. The old men who occupy power no longer reserve the right to negotiate with those who rule beyond their borders for the murder of their own children by the others' children; what the history texts call war. Do we still believe in one of the strangest blindnesses of our history? Taught, cited, praised to the skies everywhere, a certain Viennese doctor of the not-too-distant past theorized and his lieutenants popularized the dogma of the murder of the Father, while, at the same time, from 1914–45, in thirty-one years and two conflicts, a few rare old men, scattered across Europe and the world, were putting their children to death by the tens of millions. This is one of the significant contemporary bits of progress: faced with the gigantic cemeteries, who would still put up with this lie? We don't understand kamikaze acts or terrorist suicides any better. We no longer recite the verses of Corneille's *Horace* without disgust, verses which enchanted the youth from three centuries, plus my own: 'To die for one's country is such a dignified fate, That people would strive in droves to get such a fine death.'[3] Today we quite rightly find such narratives written in order to embellish piled-up corpses to be horrible. At this price, we no longer want to define ourselves exclusively as participants in a belongingness: every belongingness turns into racism. Having acquired more mastery over our singular lives, we refuse to subjugate them to an ideology covering over collective violence. We do want to yield to the delights of participation, but on the condition that the existence of the chosen collective not rob anyone of their existence. We want to abolish this death penalty. What group is worth a life?

My life: yes, I only exist if I tell a narrative of it. But we also only exist together, whatever collective we may be a member of, if we continually recount its foundation, its development, its catastrophes and its rebirths. True for two lovers, true for the city of Athens, the Roman Church, the French nation, the European continent. . . . From the beginning of my page, writing about belongingness, I have recounted my youth, our history and that of the last century. We exist, as *we*, in and by history, which I readily define as a mode of existence of the collective, whose base acts and high deeds history narrates. Without it, wouldn't the collective disappear?

---

[3]Act 2, Scene 3.

Under what conditions do you accept enlisting into some group? What investment, what motivation, what energy, in general, do you want to, can you, must you devote to some given belongingness? Another version of the questions just asked: What belief should one grant to its history? When I was recounting my life, the author of these narratives had to, as I recall, in order to create the gap that allowed this speech to unfold, surpass the death of its actor. We have just found death again at the heart of the question concerning collective history. Did this history force us to accept death, even to desire it? We now refuse it; we want to abolish human sacrifices, whose blood cements groups. I have had quite enough of my own lake of tears; I and we no longer want to believe in this bloody history; we refuse it our adherence. We would like to abolish this history of death.

Hence I find myself, we find ourselves, all humans today will no doubt soon find themselves in this new state, hesitating to sign a hitherto unseen social contract. This is what I call the crisis of belongingness: each person exists in himself and for himself, individually; an adventure that's a million years old several times over in Africa and a hundred times millenary across the world, as we have just learnt and become aware of, makes us exist as a species. I have existed as *I* for two millennia, in theory, and, in fact, for scarcely a few generations; we have all existed as the genus that is the human race since merely yesterday morning. I live, act and think in a singularly local point, me here and now; we all participate in the global fate of humanity, in the totality of the world, now inhabited in its entirety by means of the set of human – but also living, inanimate and climactic – movements.

Right in the middle of these two states, the one local and singular, the other global and specific, we no longer know how to cut up our groups, where to place our collectivities, how to choose our subsets, where and how to invest our libido of belongingness. In the centre between the fairly new *I* and a fairly new *everyone*, the *we*, an older subject than the two others, is now entering into crisis. It sustained our fathers; we are losing it. So who are we? What should we recount about ourselves? Is there a new *we*, the way the *I* and the new *everyone* appeared? But where is it to be found? Where should mine be placed? In a habitat, a profession, a language, customs and mores, social classes, rites, the flag? My niece said, 'I can no longer become a nun of God; I don't want to devote my life to a party; but I would fear even more living as the sister in crime of an enterprise.' Into what group will she want to enlist?

Wandering citizen

And what should I recount about my belongingnesses? Mobile, I inhabit Gascony with my agnates and cognati, whose language I speak, Auvergne in company with the Cantalians and the Creusois, the southeast suburb of Paris, a neighbour to street urchins and immigrants from ten countries, the Queyras with the people of the Alps, Brittany, on the sea with its sailors, Denmark and Italy with my friends, so refined, from Florence and Aarhus; Europe, therefore, but also California with its engineers and Latinos, Quebec, participating in the moving memories of New France, the Andes and its guides, Brazil with my quasi-adoptive daughter from São Paulo, Japan, in the delightful brotherhood of my translator friends, the Himalayas and its Sherpas, China, in harmony with its farmers, Lebanon and its emotional religions, Australia, magnificent in its land and humanity, Djibouti, the Malian bush and South Africa, the latter three fascinating, dangerous . . . I have lived in all these places, these groups and others still, which I loved, which I still love; I feel that I belong to each of them in some way. My body and my soul being divided like the disparate medley of colours of cultures, I have melted my culture, original, into as many solutions. I speak, quite badly I admit, a few languages . . ., participate in ancient civilizations, Cathar, Occitan, French, Spanish, Portuguese, Italian, South American, English, German . . ., Jewish, Christian, Catholic, Protestant, Orthodox, open to other religions . . . . Where should my lived and true collectivity be placed? Everywhere, nowhere, here, yonder? In the collectivity of my birth, yes; in the one in which, by chance, I will be plunged tomorrow, yes again. Fluctuating, my country lies at the intersection of countries, my culture at the intersection of cultures, my belongingness or civilization in another intersection so that, turbulent, my body haunts several crossroads. My case, common, is spreading today.

We are becoming citizens of the world, like the Stoics at the end of the ancient era; and when, in the future, we vote online, we will become: citi-netizens. I believe I am seeing the borders drawn by violent, military and criminal histories being dissolved and dying. I notice with sadness that only mediocre pressure groups hastily formed to take some power and devour small benefits are being established around me; repulsive, iniquitous, contemptible. The crisis of civilization that the West and no doubt the entire world are traversing of course comes from the process of hominization I have described, but also from the doubt gripping us today: What group should we belong to that would concern our future and carry the future of our descendants? We rarely know how to answer this question we have put on hold. Thirsting to enter a team, I searched for one without finding it. I see forming everywhere, quickly and not very numerous, friendly groups, fluctuating, with limited projects, soon vanished, temporary, as though each person, prudent, was only partly invested in it. I even remark that one becomes attached with all the more pleasure, in retirement, to a countryside with rare neighbours and a secluded horizon for having gone gallivanting, one's whole life long, among oceans and latitudes. The 'humanitary' remains, as I said, but, quite precisely, it refers to *everyone*; supernature also remains, but its kingdom lies outside this world.

Diogenes the Cynic wandered, they say, in the streets, the bearer of a lamp lit in broad daylight, crying out: I'm searching for a human! Without finding him, he sought to encounter an individual person or universal humanity, as a species or a genus. Why? Because neither of the two existed in his time and because only citizens or foreigners, slaves or free men, males or females, sailors or farmers . . . could be found in the city, all of them participants in a community that's political, social, religious, sexual, artisanal . . ., in brief, peers enlisted in belongingnesses. No *ego*, no humans. The situation has turned around one hundred and eighty degrees today: wandering, plunged in a multicoloured crowd of individuals and amid the cosmonauts of the spaceship *Earth*, I am searching for an undiscoverable community.

Lightened belongingness

I have suspected the libido of belongingness of causing a thousand ills, violence and rage. We nevertheless love, sometimes, to lodge, there, in a hut amid a black forest of conifers. Strangers to wide distances, we breathe better in a small retreat. We love parish, kinship and enrootedness.[4]

Certainly, but we are changing them. At a time when homebody agriculture is ceasing to establish the bases of our culture, we are loosening the bonds that attach us to the soil, to our altars and hearths. *Homo viator*. Lightening our belongingnesses, this is our present state and our programme: we hear this exile expressed in several languages. The Grand Narrative gives an evolutionary, temporal, hominian and immanent version of it. A hundred thousand

---

[4]This passage seems to be aimed at Heidegger, who often stayed in a small hut in the Black Forest in order to write. The word 'there' evokes the da of dasein (being-there). Enrootedness is also a Heideggerian notion. 'Small retreat' translates *réduit*, whose literal meaning of reduced stands in contrast to 'wide distances'.

years ago, our ancestors left Africa and the delights of the cradle; all of us who populate the globe are directly descended from these travellers. We cannot say we are from Gascony or from Yokohama. Here is the second version, a religious one, of this lightening. A holy lament, whose pathos doesn't belong only to the Christian religions, transforms our existence into an emigration; thrown onto foreign shores, we left the house. We weep at the memory of our origin, the Bosom of Abraham, and from our homesickness for it, hoping to return there. Whether myth or reality, illusion or deep faith, the narrative of this exile reduces our dwelling to a hotel for travellers, our familiar landscapes to foreign horizons, the totality of the same to other. We are not from here below. True life takes place elsewhere. Now the cultural version: the recent mobility of our society, deterritorialised, makes us multiply our changes of domicile. I have lived in Brest and Toulon, Clermont and Vincennes, Seoul and Tokyo, Melbourne and Brisbane, Baltimore and Stanford, Montreal and Buffalo, Djibouti and Bamako. . . . Who can say my address? The technological version: I give you my new address without referring to space any longer. By mobile phone or email, I only state numbers: we no longer inhabit places. My address no longer uses metric coordinates to situate my house but floats in the topology, without distance, of my possible travels. You can reach me wherever I may voyage. We no longer haunt the space our parents had inhabited since their African origin: this 'situation' changes what the philosophers of the past had called being-in-the-world. A new version, this one political, of this exile that's so profound that it is reflected, as one can see, in multiple facets: I feel myself to be less and less a citizen of France and more and more a citizen of the world, of course, but, in the interim, a citizen of Europe. But I feel myself to be from Europe less than I felt myself to be from France and French less than Gascon; I want to repeat, by means of this, that the merit of this originally and originarily peaceful institution consists in not demanding my life nor the lives of my grandchildren to defend its borders. This institution seeks, on the contrary, to expand them, without conquest, with welcome, without war or mourning. Our fathers built states and nations by means of conflicts, in blood; we are constructing this community with irenicism: hence its happy fragility. A joyous version, ludic and even laughable, of the same exile. In California, a British friend and I play at supporting, as we say, a soccer team, he, the team that plays in Liverpool and I, the Girodins de Bordeaux, he, an English team and I, a French one. We get a little heated about it; we hardly take it seriously; most often, we laugh about it; this allows us to invite each other to dinner right as the victories happen and to console the other if he loses. That said, the teams, made up most of the time of strangers to the city, and even to the country, the rapid succession of tournaments, the conviction that it never has to do with anything but money or even doping quickly renders this competition laughable. We play at belongingness, which is suddenly so lightened here that it brings the English Jew and the Catholic from Guyenne closer together instead of setting them into opposition. Here, lastly, is its true metaphysical version: wherever I may find myself, even on the blessed riverbanks of my childhood, even twenty thousand leagues from this place, I experience, like every human, that I am not from here, nor from there, nor from elsewhere, at any latitude. Nor from that address where the house stands that I have lived in, from time to time, for almost forty years and where, perhaps, I shall die. In the innermost part of myself, in the deepest part of my culture and my common history, in the most universal part of what makes me a human, generically speaking, these three subjects that form me live, there or here, as strangers to this place, to this building, to this space, and even to this time. I only experience a lightened belongingness. Or rather: born in the plains, I am of the sea and of the mountains; born in the countryside, I will never be of the city; but I am, as well, of the desert and of the river, of the great wide open and of summits.

I am . . . For lustra, I have hesitated, still, to use this auxiliary verb. But this word, 'auxiliary', says the very opposite of what being claims to be. Not the expression of a state, a stability, a permanence or even a unicity, but rather, stemming, it too, from the family of the verb 'to augment', it measures a possible strengthening, that increment, that variable intensity I felt just now in relating my own narrative. I am, of course, from here, from there or elsewhere: but a little, a lot, passionately, madly, sometimes, not at all, often; and, in all, more or less intensively. My dasein or being-there becomes an unstable auxiliary, a vital aid, an increase of joy, a decrement of melancholy. The auxiliary is cousins with the author, from the same family, as we have seen, of augmentation. I remain, by my narrative, the author of my life, but this or that social circle, this or that belongingness help me to write it and thus augment or diminish the intense interest of this narrative. I live better here than elsewhere, sometimes, and better elsewhere than here, often. That depends.

Stable, sharp-edged, having two values and founded, like it, on the excluded middle, extensive logic highlights and increases the logic of animal niches and belongingness. From now on, we don't so much inhabit places as we haunt them intensively. Our fluctuations ensue from the logic of fuzzy sets. At this moment, I am here with you and, in mind, in project, in regret, at the same time elsewhere with others, whom I love, as well, and whom I dream about, perhaps. *Tertium datur*. I am not. I pass. I wander. It sometimes happens that I cast anchor. Here we are, once again, embarked.

Noise and multiplicities

Diogenes and I, I said, were searching for a group, today, one not heavy with hatreds, threats and murders, but rather peaceful and light. In order to seek it, and first and foremost in order to recognize it, let's extinguish the lantern, useless during the day and deaf at night; let's open our ears more than our eyes. You always want to see. Why don't you seek to hear? What viola player doesn't know that musical execution brings the members of his quartet closer together, whereas words and sentences often separate them? Deafened by the cries of the dying, shouted out during the conflicts of my childhood, nauseated by the hymns of hatred and the biased narratives of history, I love, with pacified joy, silence. Almost all groups make noise.

I am walking towards the school playground, the public square, the fair, the train station, the stadium, the packed lecture hall in front of which I have to speak . . ., crowded places from which I am assailed by a background noise forming blankets of fog. Groups are recognized or at least announced, from afar, by this hubbub, a white noise that's all the more intense and all the more invasive as the number of participants increases. Hear there the collective equivalent of the subjective chaos of my soul, a soul burning with life and blood, emotions, joy or resentment, but also the equivalent of the objective brouhaha of calm oceans, of avalanches or hurricanes, of the telluric rumblings of earthquakes. The signals emanating from the collectivity tell the size of the assembly, its number, its joy while cheering, its indignant anger, the intensity of its violence, its noise, sound and fury. Thus I can divine, by my ears, that the recess has begun, that a brawl is growing more bitter, that a team has scored a try, that the departure of a train has emptied the platforms, that the arrival of another train has filled them, that the August vacationers have deserted Paris. From a small gathering up to another, more numerous one, I hear this hubbub grow. What does the clamour of the city signify, that sound horizon, constant like the murmuring of the sea, if not collective presence, the announcement of the *we*?

What signals emerge from this bush? No crest detaches itself, at this scale, from the cottony cloud. An attentive listener, I would like to take an even greater distance in order to try to hear a background noise whose emitters would be explosively multiplied and for which crowds and cities would be reduced to simple elements. I would thus dream of hearing the genuine noises of large collectives, the murmurings filling a large space like Europe or

France, the countless myriads of buzzing events whose directions and intensities collide and jostle one another across a continent and whose sounds astonish and scandalize millions of people or leave them cold, hatreds and loves, muffled and silent advents, protest marches, bloody accesses to power, wars, conflicts . . . interrupted with rare silent instants of peace. Can we measure, in order to learn it, the adequate distance from which to hear this gigantic hubbub, inaudible from afar, but inaudible also from anear, from which one only hears the buzzing of small assemblies? Who could, who would be able to perceive this noise and discover the distance still reached by this tremendous brouhaha emanating from the vast space in which the real multiplicities of history move, bang into each other and transform? Cosmonauts, do you hear the blue planet's noise?

The first object of the historian: these variable, Brownian, quantum, fluctuating, perceptible multiplicities, whose tone and precise sites of transmission or reception we don't assess, real disorder, but almost theoretical, poorly defined, not surrounded by a boundary, by a melodic line, barely sayable. What can we say about it? That no one has yet grasped its cacophony or symphony. Should we judge it to be inaccessible to understanding? And yet, we easily understand that there cannot be any faithful history of a collectivity, expressing as closely as possible its nature and reality, without a refined hearing of the totality of noise it produces, without an intelligent listening to this hubbub, without an exquisite sensibility to the disordered howls of its violence, to the burns of this numerous fire, to these deflagrations, to the outbursts of this disorder, to the explosive range of these meanings before all meaning, to these bushy forests of messages in every direction. Through these innumerable multiplicities, history, understood as both the unfolding of human collectivities and as a discipline, encounters large numbers, chance, the stochastic domain. Do we truly take them into consideration? We recount, while pretending to discover laws in a set that's so strictly chaotic that it at least obeys, as we shall have to say, the laws controlling physical chaos.

Just as, often, without faithfully entering into the burning chaos of our own lives or listening to the hubbub of our soul, we borrow the narrative of another public personage we admire and imitate, so history is often recited according to the form of a borrowing of the same type, whose vast distance from the actual temporal and human multiplicities is not easily measured. Except for rare exceptions, the discipline has not evolved as much as literature towards a faithful recognition of these multiplicities. I tried to do this in *Rome*.

We make so much noise that nothing happens in any other way than as a thief in the night. What decisions are we to make when faced with this crackling of an inferno? Either the resignation that only the mouths of a mob of madmen could reproduce the rumbling of this noise. The *we* would get lost in the clamour of the meaningless. Or recognize in it the rot whose stench I smelled during my adolescence, after several decades of unspeakable violence, as during this nightmare in which the following appeared:

. . . a horrible mingling
Of bruised bones and flesh dragged in the mire
And blood-soaked tatters and ghastly limbs
That devouring dogs fought over between themselves.[5]

Dreaming of events fairly similar to those with which I began my pages, Athaliah tries to make us hear the hubbub of baying roaring with violence, emanating not from a pack of fangs disgusting with blood but from a mob, strictly human, whose fury cuts into pieces the victim or victims it encounters. From the ignoble scene and its

[5]Racine's *Athalie*, Act 2, Scene 5.

torn-to-shreds brouhaha, the dream rises up; from the queen's dream, Racine draws the music of his poetry; these clamours dictate the narrative to him; from this atrocious, chaotic and sonic foundation, the tragedy arises, that deadly tragic at the foundation of our history, the history whose death I hope the dead century has achieved. Did the choir of the Greek tragedies of antiquity already express the first music to come out of this noise? From this primal hubbub, from these tiered tonalities, from these piled-up strata, so similar to the ones we met with in the formation of the soul, what god, what sages, what humanity will finally draw another history?

In my turn, I dream that, from these innumerable and noisy multiplicities, dreams, musics, representations and the cultures of the world rise up. We don't know of any collective without culture, any culture without dance, music or representation, without myth or epic, in brief, without narrative.

What singular clouds of noise cover and integrate the magnificent musics from Mali, China, the Andes, Italy . . ., singular musics, of course, but universal enough so that we can all understand them? Is the relative but real universality of music drawn from the absolute universality of chaos, from the absence of meaning of what we call white noise? I believe so. Each culture, each music, each narrative, all of them singular, all of them at the source of the pleasures of belongingness, draw from the universality in this hubbub, in this panting preceding meaning. Later, narrative, meaningful, will forget this universality. Said cultural differences launch their roots into the meaningless universal of noise.

So could I, French, calculate a kind of Fourier sum whose elements would produce Josquin des Prez, Couperin, old village tunes, Rameau, Berlioz, Ravel, Poulenc . . . horrors, 'La Marseillaise' . . .? If this sum existed, would it integrate the voices and noises of France over as many centuries? I believe so. It sometimes seems to me that I hear the unique tonality of this music, its community.

It also seems to me that the unremitting exercise of daily writing, in my language, requires listening, as though from very far away, to the harmonic *tonus* of this gigantic set. I hear the atonal base of my language before dividing it up into singing pages, paragraphs and sentences, coming in a thousand styles. Does this base emanate from our hubbub? And if I had enough ear and manifested enough listening, could I perceive, behind our brouhaha, the universal brouhaha of humanity? I believe so. It takes this limpid line, at least, to cut our furies short, to pacify our squabblings, to envelop our angers and contain our grumblings. Does the discreet clarity of this integral melody prepare another Fourier sum, one whose harmonic elements would whisper like Villon, La Fontaine, Fontenelle and Céline . . .? It also seems to me that I occasionally hear this second tonality.

I'm striving to think this sum, this sound, a kind of global harmony that would give a bit of coherence to this hubbub. The *we* would form the link of the climbing team, the vibrating rope that cuts short between the multiplicity of individual humans; my listening would integrate their noise; the sound would form the link between their voices and their entreaties; history forms the link between their autobiographies. I'm striving to think this connection, this rope, tangent or secant, this enveloping border.

So could we measure the gap between the narratives of history and this strange object, raw for listening, and also these tangential envelopes, these successive walls that seek to define, surround and master its disorder? For the historical narratives, for their part too, participate in the same quest: they seek to integrate this noise, to sum it up, to give it meaning. France's history, for example, gives meaning to our noises, sounds and national furies the way recounting my life sought to give meaning to the furies, sounds and noises of my body, my life and my time. What distance is there to be gauged between this meaning and the meaninglessness from which it emerges?

Short circuit

Let's try to measure this distance. To do so, I shall visit a region, by the sea, while consulting its map. The railroad and freeway there connect some important metropolis to some other one, not far from the coast; the highways there link two cities and the byways two villages; I can also walk on foot along the customs officers' path. Each link cuts across the fractal detail of the shoreline, whose real length, colossal, would require an interminable amount of time to reconnoitre in its minute reality. Thus, the infinity, in length, of the shorelines of Brittany is demonstrated as soon as one enters into the diversity of its rocks, crystals, molecules, atoms, towards the Brownian motion of the particles themselves. The vibration of the noise defies the infinite. We pass by the shore without seeing it by following the continuity of the rail, the asphalt, the beaten dirt, the beach . . ., by leaping over the disordered discontinuities of the real as it is. We refuse to get lost in a maze that's continually being reborn the closer it gets to the minute detail. We substitute continuities for this infinitely leafy disorder. We cut short.

Faced with the background noise emanating from my soul, I raise a lament or sing. Who am I? At first, this discontinuous chaos that noises forth, originary, original. Who am I, again? The languishing plaint, newly born, that replaces the hubbub. Who am I, lastly? The narrative that takes, in its turn, the place of this song of joy or lamentation. The plaint cuts the base brouhaha short; faithful or deceitful, the tale again cuts these meaningless musics short. It puts continuous meaning right where discontinuous, noise, sound, fury, howls, blossoming into melodies used to reign. This voice – this shortcut path – arises before bad faith. In our histories as in our souls, we always cut short; we link Nantes to Brest, Brest to Pointe Saint-Mathieu, and from there to Le Conquet via the Pointe des Renards. We avoid the shore and take the line of the road. The limit, the secant, the tangent. We eliminate, we sort, we filter. Our time doesn't flow, doesn't flow by in mass; it filters or percolates. Below certain thresholds, it doesn't flow any longer. My soul and our history are born by passing percolation thresholds.

We sort. Who would write the true history of a single yesterday? Passing to the limit above the day recounted by Joyce in *Ulysses*, Borges described the entangled madness, the mnemonic jumble the person finds himself in, who, the day after, seeks to recall the totality of what happened, in him and for him, the day before; his entire life would no longer be enough. He would find himself trapped in multiplicity, in the infinite of the noise. From this comes the vital duty of forgetting. Yes, I would give my life for the faithful memory of the day I met you: would this life be enough to recount everything? The narrative of my life cuts short. It forgets, so that I may live. Faced with infinitely more numerous materials, history cuts short; it forgets even more. It filters this or that event. It even gives what passes through the meshes of the chosen filter the name event. So it percolates, as much as time. History installs percolation thresholds. It cheats and lies, like my soul. It chooses and then marks out a railroad, a freeway, a byway, a customs officers' path, but never manages to pursue the fractal outline of the coast. It would spend an infinity of days doing so. What historian has ever attempted to narrate the duration of a group the way Joyce related his heroine's fractal falling asleep by repeating it exactly? This scholar would resemble a geographer attempting to draw up a map with a scale of 1:1, faithful to the landscape point by point. The duty of remembrance strangles life.

We retreat in the face of the discontinuous, the infinity, the noise. We link together by cutting short. The song, the voice, the narrative of my soul shorten its chaos; written or recounted, the history of historians abridges the real history that, in passing, gives out a tremendous background noise. From fossil to fossil, often separated by hundreds of thousands of years, the Grand Narrative leaps with giant strides: paleoanthropology cuts short. Who am I, who are we, what is humankind? Shortened continuous narratives. Short circuits. Abridgments. My soul, history, *Homo sapiens* and this book: successive foreshortened maps. I never declaim to you, in music or language, anything but a short circuit, finite and continuous, percolating over the noise, discontinuous and infinite. I will have never finished telling you everything, I will still be trying to write it in the article of my death. I find myself, we find ourselves, quite forced to remain with the narrative. With the breviary.

How are we to gauge our and my fidelity to the real, deaf and mute, but rustling beneath the words? Historians or memorialists, are you speaking true or false? Does this question even have any meaning, since, to answer it, we would have to compare a finite segment, continuous and short, with the gigantic chaos of an infinite and stochastic sea? No criterion exists to think such a relationship.

Far from history explaining literature, as in what we call the historical approach to literature, literature, quite the contrary, ought to explain history, by gradually unveiling the wildly chaotic multiplicities preceding the emergence of a collective consciousness, preceding the emergence of local languages, preceding the emergence of musics. Just as literatures slowly evolve towards a grasp of this chaos, lying in the closest proximity alongside self-consciousness, could history gradually drift towards a grasp of such multiplicities? Out of faithfulness or concern for the truth, shouldn't the historian listen – but with what ear? – to the enormous background noise emitted by the collectives whose fateful line he is attempting to sketch? From the city, the port, the road, groups and so on, noise is given out. Number is never silent.

What music, what voices shoot up from this brouhaha? Who heard it? Hear, O Israel. Ephphatha, be opened.[6] Religions have heard them or included them for a long time, letting muezzin and bells, Angelus and tolling sound above the villages and the suddenly contemplative harvesters. Gathered together for Pentecost, the

---

[6]Mk 7.34.

apostles heard a raging wind and received tongues of fire before speaking or singing in languages: Wouldn't you say that the Acts follow, for a collective and quasi literally, the schema (drawn twice, inside my consciousness and inside our collective) of the formation of language starting from heat and noise?

For these carillons, sirens and orchestras, rare in the past, contemporary times have recently substituted the thunder of engines and the constant music in the railway stations and airports, the stores and the streets, in every house, while from the ears of the passers-by, walkmen hang like bells around the necks of cows in a meadow: *Homo clarinans*. This soul-stealing noise, as I have said, sticks an already formatted collective at the centre of the individual by expelling inwardness, and therefore puts an already born *we* in the place of the *I* and of a *we* that we would freely form. We will no longer be able to recount our lives according to our own laments but only those of our models, enchained, enslaved, swept along by songs formatting everyone's soul, impelled by examples imposed by the most uneducated dominant people in history. Opinion drives thought out; format freezes freedom; fashion expels invention. Since music descends more deeply into souls than propaganda does into minds, we format the inwardness of individuals from the inside: How will they protect their self-containment, how will they invent the new, how will we get out of convention? This is the emergence of an orthopaedic *we*, artificial, imposed, in the triple sense of impost, imposture and obligation. More effective than ten police forces, this appalling servitude pursues us from shops to restaurants so as to suppress our possible noises of revolt. I love music, I hate this music.

The nine Muses construct the walls of the black box

We live in the grip of the Muses. They gave, it was once said, gentleness to kings by dictating words and sounds to them that calmed disputes and re-established peace. The traditions of Thrace put them in contact with Dionysia and Orphism, dark and infernal cults. The appalling war of the gods against the Titans gave rise to their first songs. It suffices, Hesiod claimed, for a singer, their servant, to celebrate the exploits of a man of the past for a listener overwhelmed with grief and cares to forget them. Guided by Apollo Musagetes, that lyre player who slit the throat of Marsyas and impaled him in order to flay him, the Muses cover over the noise, the sound and the fury. How? By means of dance and music, tragic or comic performances, astronomy, the harmony of the spheres, all of them prior to epic poetry and history, all of them lastly daughters of Mnemosyne.

From the beginning of this book, I haven't said anything else, but in different words, abstract ones, sometimes concrete, clumsy and not easy in comparison to these images and statues gleaming with intuition, whose depth and range I suddenly grasp. The symbolic procession of the nine ancient sisters, who were made into cold allegories by our stupidity and painted or sculpted on the pediments of academies, in fact describes, and with a sovereign rigour, the successive layers necessary to dominate the incomprehensible background noise and the bayings of fury that come out of the black box of collectivities, no doubt also the successive layers necessary to subdue the deafening fracas emanating from the black box of the *me*, the successive layers necessary to hear me, myself, and to hear each other.

I am describing two black boxes: *me* and *us*. Who am I? A box, whose form, if it exists, stays stable, although empty, and from which nothing comes out but a background noise, black. Who are we? Another box, one having unstable forms, from which, again, a background noise comes out, black, a background noise whose number prevents understanding. These two torrential clouds cause fear. Inside me, it causes me anxiety and, in the surroundings, terrifies us. Since the second one, millions of times noisier, has no periphery, we cannot immediately put it in a box. Its borders must first be made clear. It must be delimited so that nothing can go beyond it, and, consequently, be defined as a box. Its content is of no consequence, incomprehensible and risky in any case, the important thing remaining to draw its contours, its margins, its edges. Where does this noise come from? From our team, from our army, from our technology, from our city. Our music, our bloody hymns, our songs, our tragedies, the memory of our short past, our history . . . try to muffle it, to forget it, to calm it. Behold: I recognize my book.

In which I shall now continue the list of the Muses, about whom it has been recounted that here or elsewhere, named the Pierides or the Charites, they found themselves three or six or seven before reaching the count of nine. They constructed the box for the gigantic fracas of the Battle of the Titans, drew its boundary, enclosed it within successive barriers; many such barriers were necessary to hold up under the pressure – dionysiac, orphic, lethal – of the sound and the fury; it would be necessary to reinforce it with three, six, seven or even nine bulkheads. What purpose do you think dance served, which Louis XIV himself claimed to be the ballet master of, amid the quarrels of the courtiers in Versailles and the distant brouhaha of the discontented people? What purpose does René Girard's imitation serve and the pantomime of every era, peer pressure, faced with raging violence? What purpose do chorale, unison and polyphony serve? To expel those who sing out of tune, to regulate the tonal thorns and the differences between tessitura with each other? And epic poetry, tragedy, history? They all, like the others, serve the purpose of constructing barriers and cutting short.

Look at them, these nine women, at continual work – exhausting, necessary – incessantly sealing up the leaks of this box, of this barrel of the Danaides with its broken staves, closing up the leaks of the hull, of this personal or collective cavern out of which the madness of the anxious clamours come. Say what purpose culture serves; unwise are those who firmly believe it serves no purpose at all. It saves our skin and, first and foremost, our ears. It attempts to plug up this well of terror and to guide us beyond its surroundings. We wouldn't survive without the multiplicity of its sounds and of its narratives. At least, we wouldn't hear each other; at most, we would kill one another. This is the genuine substructure of our societies.

Faced with the box and its major risks, the nine Muses and we work, relentless, at building dikes, at strengthening walls, at reinforcing bulkheads, sometimes even by going, loyal and courageous, as close as possible to the background noise. Polyhymnia devotes herself to pantomime; Terpsichore dances; Erato directs choral song; Euterpe plays the flute; Urania contemplates and calculates the landscaped harmony of the heavens; Melpomene weeps at tragedy; it would be better to laugh at comedy, says Thalia; no, even better would be the epic poetry of Calliope; we lastly prefer history, Clio. Written or oral, these narratives, products of the latter cited Muses, emanate from music, emitted by the first cited Muses; but this music, which furthermore names all of the Muses, emanates from the thunder of war and the incomprehension that is noise. I haven't said anything else; my book is deciphering the myth of the Muses, which, in return, illuminates it. From having understood the urgency of their work and the intelligence of their genealogy, I will no longer make fun of those draped women with their grandiloquent and icy poses that render public vainglory ugly with foolishness. From now on, I admire them; I ought to have entitled my book: *Hymn to Music*.

Music everywhere, music always, the work of the Muses is in full swing in our society of the spectacle. Far from having held the infrastructure in the past, today economics holds it from having bought culture.

Pythia and passion

Another ancient image that's as dazzlingly evident: seated above a crevasse in the ground, from which eddies and vapours emanated, the Pythia of Delphi would rave. She expressed these agitations in oracles, going from these noises to gurglings. The priests would translate her incoherent delirium into verses. The conduct of peoples depended, it is said, on decisions inspired here. Do you think we have changed this? The media have seized the nine Muses, Pythia of Delphi and her interpreters.

What function does a politician fill, sitting on the throne of some power? His seat plugs a hole in the black box. Should this potentate stand up, this action will open this inspection hole through which the noise, sound and fury of the group will pass, a group which, by its acclamation, brought him over this pit from which these agitation noises are heard to howl. The foundation of power plugs up this hole, bricks it up, closes it up, seals it off, repairs it, caulks, blocks, muzzles, gags it. Inseparable twins, the politician and his media translators don't so much know the group as they prevent anyone from knowing it. Like the Muses did, they dance it, sing it, evoke it, perform it, dramatize it . . . in sounds, images and sentences, tragedies and comedies. They do nothing but repress the fury of the crowd. We cast our votes and open up parliaments to cover over this uproar with narratives. Our need of power can be measured by the fear our noise causes us.

Other images and sounds, more modern and even truer. I take the earthquake that followed the death of Jesus Christ as seriously as the descent into the underworld that preceded his Resurrection. Peaceful, the narrative of the Gospels enters into the Passion, violent and harsh, traverses tribunals and accusers, and then plunges into the furies of the masses and the background noise of the world. After the gentleness of the Eight Beatitudes, the rabble pounces, the victim cries out with his death throes, lastly the earth itself shakes. It opens up and allows passage to the dark realm. Narrative, tragedy, clamours. In comparison to the canonic sequence of the box's walls, whose order is becoming familiar to us, music has failed to appear. Several composers didn't fail to write *Passions*, and, at the end of *The Seven Last Words of Christ*, Haydn translated the earthquake into sounds that are a fair bit disharmonic. Rameau, Vivaldi . . . so many others as well attempted to make these tempests and battles be heard, tempests and battles that Fellini translated into images in the unforgettable *Orchestra Rehearsal*, in which sound and noise, the group, its cohesion and its furious disintegration, the symphony and the destruction of the walls or bulkheads of the box in which the orchestra plays follow one another, as in this book: the *we* subject, its life and its death.

In the Gospels, antiquity (several images of which we have just admired) died. On the Cross expired the victim of a judicial mistake, like there are so many. But this victim died to ensure the group its cohesion for the last time. Where does the noise emanate from? From a crisis. A collective scatters into opposing clans; the *we* subject becomes split up. To reconstruct it, the simplest but cruellest operation consists in killing a victim together. By means of this sacrifice, the group, the *we* subject, exists anew. After the Passion, this operation lost its effectiveness. It would no longer work. There would no longer be, in principle, any *we*'s formed in this murderous fashion. All such *we*'s were expelled into antiquity. Better: antiquity would be defined as the sacrificial era constituted, in this way, from such *we*'s. We have perhaps only become aware of this today. It would take two thousand years to digest this message. We had recommenced, endlessly, the same hideous operation, but in vain. These sacrifices no longer worked and would never work again. We rejected this bloody tatter, become ineffective. We would no longer water our furrows with this impure blood. This *we* died, on Golgotha, and no longer even lay mummified in a tomb. From this cenotaph, from this empty tomb, indeed, from this memoryless place, the Son of Man was risen: that is, an individual and the human universal, the two subjects Diogenes was looking for, himself named Son of God, and which he didn't find because his antiquity knew nothing, in fact, but *we*'s. This *we* had just died. This subject had just expired. This particular noise had been heard for the last time. The earth trembled from it.

The death of Jesus Christ marks the precise moment when the ancient situation was turned around and our situation appeared, the one these pages are describing. What is antiquity? The era when there was nothing but *we*'s, without any *ego*, without universal humanity. Out of the three subjects, only one existed. The dead *we* brings about the two modern subjects: an *I* and a genus, the individual and the universal. Out of the three subjects, two remain. Contemporary times repeat this date.

Chance bifurcations and necessities in return

As you remember, by cutting short, autobiography intended to paint a portrait, a profile or silhouette appearing on the background of this noise; likewise, history cuts out an extract from the innumerable thicket of the past. How?

Since the morning, I have been hiking in the mountains, below timberline, along a trail whose bends sometimes follow the contour lines. When I turned around this morning, I saw a woods of Norway spruce and, at the bottom of the valley, the village I had just left, beneath the steeple of its modest church. In ascending a continuous slope for several hours and turning around again, I contemplate, behind me, a wide landscape of mountains, in which the Écrins chain is unfurled, with, in front, Pelvoux glacier; in the foreground, in a meadow lower down, surrounded by its sheepdogs, a herd of sheep is idling beneath the noontime sun.

The hamlet and the forest have disappeared. What I see of the spots I have just passed depends on the direction the trail is now following. A curve is enough to transform the previous landscape. There, the woods and the village; here, herd and glacier.

Familiar in space and for our movements, this change of perspective is reproduced with time, for which we are less inclined to admit that the past, too, depends on our bifurcations. In reading with astonishment and sometimes to the point of scandal what my children learn about my youth in the history books, I no longer understand my youth; their youth already doesn't have the same Second World War as me; it has bifurcated a hundred times with the pill and the internet. Thanks to the appearance of our long-distance communications, we remember the fires lit by the Carthaginians, from Pantelleria, in Sicily, to keep Hannibal up to date with the news and to receive the news of his battles against the Romans. We laugh or we are scandalized at the ancestral moralities because we no longer suffer from the daily pains undergone by our fathers, whose patience had forged rules for practising to endure them. The invention of genetics allowed Mendel's articles to be opened up again, which physiologists hadn't read for more than sixty years; the monk with his peas didn't belong to biology's past during the era when Claude Bernard had triumphed; he entered into our past with genetic coding. Without Christianity, would we be able to read, in the Old Testament, the figures of the New Testament Pascal detected there? When I was writing my book on *Rome*, how many times did I burst into laughter upon reading, regarding the same ancient city, Scottish or American Southern authors I caught describing contemporary Texas or Victorian Scotland rather than ancient Latium or, in other instances and perhaps my own, the French countryside rather than the banks of the Tiber? We no longer have the same antiquity, the same Bible, the same French Revolution, the same science memories as any of our predecessors. In brief, the past is renewed with each of our newnesses; in rereading it in a retrograde fashion, our present realigns it at will.

Yet, if, in slipping off the trail, I broke my leg and the rescue helicopter lifted me away vertically from my position, I would undoubtedly see, behind me, the Barre des Écrins, several woods, of firs or of larches, the adjacent valleys and their four or five villages, their town halls, hotels, chapels. . . . Every bend of the trail had selected, in this massif, alignments and perspective views, of which I would have, from above, a view of the whole, or rather of a subset, for if the apparatus hoisted me higher still, I would discover how much that first view still cut out a landscape from a wider whole. The global image of the Earth our cosmonauts let us see could give a limit to this ascent: from so high, does the landscape verge on a map?

The image of a trail suggests a realignment. The fact of recounting suggests this even more, with the line of the narrative running from a prelude to the end, the way a river goes from its sources to the delta; its course has a bed and tributaries, the way a narrative has its principal impetus and its bifurcations. History presents a fate that seems irresistible when this fate is read from downstream to upstream. Every time the fateful flow is jostled and bifurcates due to this, it reorders its past, it filters from the past the elements suitable for conditioning what follows, whatever the nature that may be presented by what follows. Some given revolution or conflict searches for its causes upstream and can't help but find them among the chaotic pile of past things; thus, whatever the new direction the course in question may take, this course will always discover, before this new direction, solutions to the causal questions the new direction asks. For, innumerable and endless like the landscape from just now seen from high enough up, the past contains everything that can become, at will, the set of causes or conditions of any future outcome. Similar to a problem with an infinity of solutions, history is never mistaken. The historian even less so. We can never falsify the first nor convict the second of error. Outside science, since non-falsifiable, history remains captivating for the libido of belongingness, which abhors error. No one can falsify it because its ultimate reference contains the continuous infinity of noise. Thus, its past narrative appears as a quasi-necessary set of causal chains, even though every bifurcation before was freely played as though at random.

Whether it's a question of autobiography, history or even of the Grand Narrative, how are we to define this narrative itself? By the fact that it contains, for better and for worse, these causes and these choices, chance and necessity. To talk about humanism, I have chosen this genre because it enjoys this synthesis.

Could we collect the totality of the past without this obligation to extract from it one or more sequences? Get the photograph of the massif and valleys, at the limit the photograph of the globe, instead of walking along there step by step, by roads and trails? For someone to fathom or understand this past, a collection, a global recollection, would still have to take the form of an order, whether linear, serial, flat or illustrated, in volume and in relief, even multiple, is of no consequence. But, amid the dense and disordered set of the given, this ordering, necessarily, eliminates. So the totality before filtering indeed resembles raw disorder, a chaos full of noise, sound and fury. In other words, the observer that's present and his concern for observing introduces an order and a filter such that he loses the infinite noise. Again, Orpheus cannot turn around towards Eurydice without her disappearing.

I repeat, the problems of knowing the collective – who are we? – rediscover elements already met with in the internal knowledge of the *me* – who am I? – in which another chaos, maybe even the same one, was emitting background noise. For I can always find a secret intention inside me, unavowed, unconscious or in bad faith, whose nature and intensity will be able to, at will, cause, explain or justify some new action, surprising to those close to me, and which, sometimes, stupefies even myself. When I bifurcate, I turn around and recreate a new past, amid an inextricable massif. Chance and necessity are tied together in the present.

The past proposes an open and indefinite set of possible candidates to causality. The word 'candidate' expresses a possible choice, but its root also designates the purest white. An example: it seems that a group of people from Paris stormed the Bastille on 14 July 1789. Supposing King Louis XVI, for this or that reason, had continued to rule all the way up until a ripe old age, a certain revolt having expired before he did, the demolition of the prison building would have become a simple detail, neglected by historians, in the redevelopment of a square. Once accomplished, this event offers the eye of successors a kind of white hold, adaptable to anything that may follow, like a domino that's adjustable to any number or like piles of metal waiting in an unfinished building. What happened in the past and recently forms a set of such free branchings. According to its direction, what follows colours one such branching, as it chooses and pleases, according to its own colour, in fact determines it, giving it a status of reality. It is often said that the future is open, virtual, brimming with possibilities. This can be said of the past. Among the immensity of its disordered chaos, the future chooses and, in return, stabilizes its choice. The narrative only appears linear if you turn around, at a crossroads.

Would I say the same thing about my soul, brimming with possible candidates for the narrative I draw out of myself, a chaotic set of virtuals offering themselves, in a disordered hubbub, to the multiple choices of my discourse, the way, on the Galapagos Islands, male frigate birds stretch out and, candidates for lovemaking, swell up their crop towards the females flitting about them? A white noise, they say, accompanies chaos and disorder. Personal or collective, all our histories emanate from this whiteness, from these possible candidates.

Is the Grand Narrative itself, lastly, going to play the role of the cosmonauts' photograph?

The retrograde movement of the chaos

Inventions, discoveries, these are good news, unexpected bifurcations. We historians of science, for example, have a lot of trouble interpreting their dynamic. When the Schrödinger equation or the computer came into the world, newnesses came to be that few previous things had heralded. Why? Because the researcher doesn't know anything about what he is going to find before finding it, since if he did know, he would have already found it. The person who discovers this formula or that planet rarely knows he is searching for this planet or that formula. We have endless trouble putting ourselves upstream of the discovery because we already know its content. Algebra without Vieta or biology before Mendel belong to universes that have vanished forever, which the new idea had closed. Can we likewise form some idea of the state of affairs on 15 July 1789, when the Bastille, already stormed, hadn't yet heralded the French Revolution? Men of the Ancien Régime, Turgot, Necker or Louis XVI didn't foresee anything of the kind. And now we say, easily, that they must have guessed, at least a little, what rupture they were advancing towards. Nothing ever goes where one thinks it will. The least pebble can cause a slender flow to diverge that's destined to vanish or to become gigantic. Familiar with the downstream, we believe the upstream contains in potentiality the elements that flower downstream. But we observe these elements only when they flower. Historical narrative is conjugated in the future perfect.

Livy had an easy time of it making the first kings of Rome discourse on the Empire's greatness to come. They were almost as ignorant of it as I am ignorant of what the state of the world will be on the morning of the day after tomorrow. Even more, the Romulus or Numa Pompilius he talked about no doubt have nothing to do with the real individuals to the same degree that the Rome Livy talked about has nothing to do with the first village, weak enough to fear its neighbours, the Albans, Etruscans or Sabines. We never talk about anything but worlds that have been transformed from top to bottom by their futures, in such a way that these worlds have vanished.

Contemporary chaos theory clarifies what Bergson called the retrograde movement of the true, no doubt under the influence of Poincaré, certain of whose equations had already described this view of things. Because we don't master the initial conditions of a motion, the present, this theory says, cannot determine its future or futures. Unpredictable and contingent, it can bifurcate from the estimated trajectory. Conversely, if we consider the past from the present, then everything appears determined: it easily announces its sequence. Deterministic from this retrograde point of view, the curve becomes contingent in considering the future. Mechanical systems make rigorous the common experience that we can never guess what awaits us, while the past appears to us as coherent. How, out of ideology, can we still put forward laws of history, while mechanists, faced with systems that are infinitely simpler, have abandoned them for more than a hundred years? Ignorance of initial conditions makes the future unpredictable, say the hard sciences; this is an education that's immediately applicable to human multiplicities: we never master every condition and predict nothing. The claim to there being laws of history ought to vanish before the question: if there are any, then predict. This is what the mechanist or the astronomer does, whose predictions have to do with figures and motions, solstices and eclipses. This is what even the sciences lagging in prediction hope for, watching out for warning signs of volcanic eruptions or earthquakes. But whatever predictions these sciences may succeed in making, the fact remains that chaos theory can suddenly contradict them. Thus, even in the hardest sciences, contingency has entered into necessity.

For sudden inventions or other news, we never expound, afterwards, anything but necessary conditions. Without them, nothing would happen, of course; but with them, once more just as necessary, nothing would happen either. The entire economy of the world and its prosperities will never make this discovery or that work of art appear. Only sufficient conditions would launch the sequence. Masterful or mediocre, a hundred explications are overflowing with necessary conditions, but none of them yet has laid its hands on sufficiency. The human and social sciences deploy a fine talent in the search for conditions. But how does it happen that the same, or at least similar, conditions – abusive father, castrating mother, low social class, abusive childhood – produce, here, a hoodlum and, there, a generous person, in one circumstance, a mathematician, in some other, an illiterate? How are we to find the sufficient condition, as light as a feather, as silent as the air?

Sufficiency and necessity together are part of the initial conditions. Since Hadamard and Poincaré, we have known – Duhem had already said this – that knowing them completely goes largely beyond the framework of possible enterprises. However much the historian may furiously work in the archives, interview witnesses, should they still exist, never will he come to the end of the infinite detail. This multiplicity looms above him, and, already, the narratives of the contemporaries form a partial filter of the set of facts. In whatever way they may remain, the witnesses of the past only reach an order far below events, whose infinite set noises forth. But we can enjoy the narrative.

Landscape

I shall return to after the death of Christ. By the earthquake's fracas, the earth enters, if I may, from outside, into the collective's inward box. Narrative, tragedy, the sound and noise of history don't only concern women, men, children and groups. Above, in my egotistical narrative, I also encountered landscapes, seas and mountains. I don't live alone in the world and don't recount only my solitary adventure. No matter how much my discourse may put me in the position of being a champion, the fact remains that the environment does not reduce me to pure ipseity. Many other people weave their narratives into the weft of my own, and the whole of the fabric takes place in the world. Walls, cities and bridges, deserts and countrysides. Would Robinson himself have survived without his island, springs, plants and goats? The landscape, caves and rocks, animals and trees are not laid about as the décor for his life but are part of his history, as indispensable actors for his hunger and his rest; his pathetic soul reverberates, multiplied, in Echo Valley, whose walls send his voice back to him.

Yes, the landscape becomes unstuck from the décor; theatrical, the latter, made of stucco, pasteboard and colouring, in imitation of the real, can, indifferent, vaguely adapted, staged, enframe a hundred narratives, a framework quasi independent of the story being told. No, the earth, fauna and flora participate in our agrarian adventure; the sea and beach guide our travels or lead them astray; the desert makes the Bedouin thirst; the cliff face can kill the mountaineer. Deprived of landscape, the narrative – narcissistic, social, political, of the city and the apartment – coils itself, acosmic, around loves and rivalries, without any other danger than intraspecific murder. Of course, we risk our hide and the violence of others there, but neither hierarchy, nor friendship, nor tears nourish. We need heating and shelter, food and drink. A necessary condition for our survival, the landscape acts in the narrative, can annihilate it, reorient it, cause a thousand new developments.

In passing, let's celebrate the aforementioned social sciences, to which we owe a thousand fine narratives of ethnology and sociology, in addition to history. Thanks to them, we have lost narcissism and racism; thanks to them, we invite others and foreigners to our table the way we invited ourselves to their tables; anyone who does not cultivate such exchanges cannot understand a thing about today, yesterday, the rest of time or the rest of space. But I deplore the education of philosophers, politicians and journalists in their exclusive school. Deprived of the contribution of the harder sciences, the contemporary forum ends up believing that social relations alone cause us to live and nourish us. Necessary conditions, of course, not sufficient. The world is absent from the discourses that weave our opinions, decisions and certainties. Who now confronts the everyday: cows, wheat, seas and cod, this iron, these woods or these rocks that give our hands calluses? When the hard withdraws under the grip of the soft, no one has their feet on the earth any more. Is there no longer any landscape except an audiovisual one? TV weather forecasts replace snow, ice and thunderstorms, which are only experienced now, risks included, during vacations in Arcadia. Apartment thinkers talk about words, signs and codes; their acosmism erases objects, living things, the universe and the wind. Our narrative no longer concerns anything but us. No, the landscape we inhabit frequents us.

Worse, the nature/culture distinction opened up when we invented it, a free field for unrestrained conquests; an object without a subject, said nature became a place without rights, a treasury to be used up without compunction, and a trash can to be filled up without shame, to which our incremental desires would help themselves and into which our excremental garbage would be thrown. In front of the pure décor, we are only interested in humans and the ardours of their greed, envy, dominance. Since our human, social, political, historical narratives do not take the landscape into account, they blindly pillage it; since our cultures give themselves the right to say that nature is without rights, they defile and destroy it. From *The Troubadour of Knowledge* and *Paysages des sciences* to *The Natural Contract*, I have attempted, without making myself heard, to put the world and its knowledge back into their place, in the education of the individual (so that his own narrative can become balanced again, thanks to the things themselves), as well as in history and philosophy (so that an age responsible for the world can finally arise). We exist in the universe and populate the planet on which each of us lives confronted with its landscape.

Of course, things, more and more, depend, for the most part, on us. Begun with *Homo erectus*, the inventor of fire, the confrontation with what did not depend on us ends with victories that are so precise and other probable defeats that the current *sapiens sapiens* doesn't know if it must put itself on the side of the victors or of the vanquished. Victorious, it also worries. For we depend, now, on things that, quite precisely, depend on us, on the effects of our victories. Another such triumph and we shall be ruined, responded King Pyrrhus to those who were congratulating him for having beaten the Romans at Herculea and then at Asculum, but at the cost of enormous losses. We don't always realize the weaknesses our power leaves in its wake; we don't always realize our Pyrrhic victories. Intelligent, effective, the parasite wins its battles day after day, but it always ends up losing the war when, precisely, its hosts dry up. So now, but I have said this enough, we have to treat nature as a symbiont and no longer as a treasury, and, here, as a landscape and no longer as a décor.

I will begin again. Who are we, together? A lattice, the text of a thousand narrations, our history, our culture. This begins with the secrecy of our loves, the narrative of our encounters and its confluence in history, family traditions, portraits of ancestors and the photo album of our children, the memories exchanged during major holidays; this is formed in the annals of cities, of provinces, of the nation; this, all of a sudden, is called, for example, the *History of France*, the history Michelet related, whose narrative describes, first and foremost, the landscapes of the land. What is Paris? Its history in the Seine Valley. What is France? Its history and its geography.

To the question – who am I? – biographies answer in ten literary genres; to the question – who are we? – the answers, parallel, modulate history, variably, since literary genres are mixed up in this too. Epic history or novelized, idyllic or theatrical, militant, hagiographical . . ., but I am revolted by those that scorn geography. However egotistically I may compose it, my autobiographical narrative cannot help but to take into account the air I breathe, my food, therefore the land and the climate. Young and poor, I wasn't able to finish a book because I was cold. The collective isn't only made up of individuals; pure politics and sociology aren't exhausted by the social fact, which is always supported by a landscape [*paysage*] that plays, via the intermediary of farmers [*paysans*], an active role in the narrative. There can be no narrative without its land [*pays*], and no Grand Narrative without the Universe.

The history of the Australian Aborigines cannot be understood without a land, a fauna and a flora that didn't permit them to invent agriculture or livestock breeding; as a result, we Eurasians or Central Americans, farmers since the Neolithic, understand, thanks to their misadventure, that the surrounding humus, mammals and grasses were acting as much as we were and always act in our historical actions. Their contribution in food sculpts us. This geography can play a role without the actors being aware of it: how many thinkers, how many Greek historians or inhabitants of the Middle East perceived, in antiquity, the damage caused by deforestation around the perimeter of the Eastern Mediterranean? Who, save Noah, right before the Flood, heard the colossal noise of the Bosporus in the process of bursting under the pressure of the new flood waters from the Sea of Marmara?[7] I repeat, this landscape isn't to be confused with a décor; it influences us, plays a role in the narration, even if, long victorious in the Pyrrhic style, we no longer integrate it into the narration directly. Without geography,

---

[7]Serres wrote the Sea of Azov. I presume this was a mistake.

there can be no collective history. Geography returns behind our backs.

Behind our backs . . .

Once citizens of the world, the Stoics of antiquity formulated their wisdom by distinguishing the things that depended on us from those that didn't depend on us. We fabricated ploughshares, exchanged wheat, navigated by sail, managed a herd of sheep, a colony of bees, our family, the city . . ., whereas there was nothing we could do about the world or the climate, the hour of my birth or the hour of my death. In a pinch, I could make myself the master of myself, of my tools and of my acts, of my feelings, maybe even the master of my close relations, here and now, not of geography and the Universe, always and everywhere. We held certain systems, finite, local and short, in our hands, whereas we were living plunged in other systems, global and lasting, maybe infinite, of which we were a part and which, in their turn, manipulated us. In the first case, causing; in the second case, caused.

But, today, these global things: the living, their evolution and disappearance, including our own disappearance, whether personal or collective; humanity in its entirety and its fate; the planet itself, its heat, its winds, the level of its seas and its habitability . . ., yes, these things, too global to become objects for our predecessors, which they had to allow to follow their fate and into whose hands their own destiny was placed, these things, as I was saying, now depend on our expert technologies, even on our everyday actions. We no longer shape merely our implements, our internal consciousness, our immediate surroundings and sometimes our neighbourhood, but also space and geographical and biological time. Our influence goes beyond stable things taken in their instantaneity so as to attain wide long-term systems. By changing scale, our objects have changed; from the local to the global for the expanse, and, for duration, from the instant and even history to evolution. Consequently, as I have said elsewhere, we [*nous*] now depend on things that depend on us [*nous*]. Let's now seek to know what this *we* signifies, curiously said twice.

Consider this: we held the old objects (easy to handle) thrown in front of us, perceiving their bounds in space and across time. Yet, not only do we know how to build what I have in the past called world-objects, which exceed the aforementioned bounds – thermonuclear bombs, effluents from certain industries, communication systems, artificial satellites, biotechnologies . . . – but the world itself, water and air, life and time, birth and death, climate and duration, have become, in their turn, for us, objects. Whom do we hold them in front of?

Consider this as well: local and mobile, the old objects could become objects of exchange, whose circulations wove the collective; there can be no group without these objects, and no society without exchange. But owing to their global dimension, the new objects are now, most often, outside exchange. One can seize springs, fixed and locatable, but not steal the vagaries of the rains. Or rather, the main stake, tomorrow, will revolve around these questions: Yes or no, will the air, the climate, birth, death . . . enter into market circulation? I wager no; if yes, a total war eradicating humanity would ensue. With local objects, multicoloured societies arise; with global objects, unitary humanity arises. This is what a consistent realist or materialist would say.

These new objects, outside exchange, affect us, worry us, oppose us, gather us. First piece of news: it's no longer a matter of the same objects; second piece of news, it's no longer a matter of the same *we*. With this pronoun, transparent to their eyes and almost forgotten in their precept, the ancient Stoics designated their own scattered group of rich, learned and wise citizens, their cities too, maybe even their empire, in brief, collectives compatible with the finite range of their tools. To fabricate ploughs, a family is sufficient; to assemble a ship, a village of fisherman; to build palaces, a city is needed; to line up an army or organize an administration, a state. To the size of an object, to the scale of a project, to the evolution of a work correspond the size, scale and evolution of a group and the duration of its history.

Today, we are more expert and less wise, perhaps, than the Stoics of yesteryear, more powerful and nevertheless weaker, masters and slaves, crazy and reasonable, multiplied, irresponsible, separated from one another by a thousand opaque customs, as usual. Of course, everything now depends on us, but we tragically depend on the disparate and polemical dispersion of this *we* I have just said was in crisis. However, such a chaos of differences tends to become recruited into unity. What new group do these world-objects give rise to?

Alas, we haven't yet succeeded, at least for the moment, in setting up a global institution suitable for mastering the grasp, the management and the evolution of these world-objects, which are no longer merely diffuse around us and 'causing', but also thrown in front of us and almost as 'caused' as the local objects formerly were, small in size and short in duration; in any case, caused by us and causes, in part, of our future. These global and lasting systems seem to me to recruit a new group of subjects, a new *we*. If they exist, a collective must definitely have produced them; for example, someone must have made the air that we breathe and the water we drink cloudy. Conversely, we must definitely also, and urgently, deal with drinking and breathing tomorrow. In other words, we will gather together less by our own decision or own good will in order to manage these world-objects than said objects, by their span and strength, will inevitably gather us in the end, have even already gathered us. Everything happens as though the objects were recruiting, were gathering, almost of themselves, subjects. This new objectivity produces, of itself, a new community of subjects, one as global as the size of these world-objects, one as wide for space, of course, but also referring to a vastly longer duration. I mean by this that the origin and evolution of this new human collective are going to take us infinitely farther back, from today on, than history in the ordinary sense, that of writing, tools, families, cities, nations, continents, the aforementioned civilizations.

Hominescent, this new time refers to the adventure of hominization. We are losing our links with the local and short histories of our specifically cultural past. When we say *these new things now depend on us*, do we know what we are saying? Do we divine that a *we* that lives, inhabits and organizes a space, a time, a sociology, a culture, a politics . . . in a new way is being formed, one bearing no relation to what the old *we*'s, diverse and multicoloured, frequented, did, said, taught or learnt? Small or large stable and unstable systems, the groups that formed our diverse histories, on the one side, and this new *we*, on the other, are separated from each other the way two eras are distinguished from each other that are as different as the geological times in which the Seine flowed under the Mirabeau Bridge, from its source to the English Channel, and the times when its basin didn't exist, sleeping on plates from another age. I no longer search for the sources of what we became upstream from the Mirabeau Bridge, under which the Seine counts a time that's too short for my new loves, rather I ask them of the physics of the earth, whose narrative tells me that in ancient eras another time unfurled, without river or plain, of which we retain traces that concern our future.

In sum, if 'these things' now depend on us, and if, in return, we are beginning to depend on 'them', we have to clarify what both *these things* and *we* mean. We have seen and named the former with as much amazement as anxiety ever since they took on global spatiotemporal dimensions, world dimensions, universal dimensions: earth, water, air, the fires of energy, life . . .. But, we, faced with them, what are we becoming? How are we to organize this new community that is now referred to objects that are as gigantic, to spaces that are as wide and to times that are as long as those of these objects? Do we realize the immense consequences of this widening of these differential ruptures?

'Who am I?' I said, to start with. I will recount again, if you like, the narrative of my life. Next, who are we? Or rather, who were we up until this very morning? Answer: we loved to think, with good reason not too long ago, that we were constituted by the narrative of our histories. We enjoyed the ancestral chronicles of France and Navarre; we never cease building museums, like those boats, with stopped engines, that still continue under their own momentum; our Portuguese friends dream of Magellan and Vasco da Gama; every group still sings the narrative of its history. Thus I still do. D'oc and d'oïl, the distinctive style of rare eponymous geniuses has formed my language, from which I draw three narratives, my own, that of my belongingness, lastly the one I am endlessly trying to invent. . . . My language has made my flesh, and my flesh has made books in my language. What rending must I now live through? Must I change flesh? I fear this and hope for it and think so. What do we now have in common with Louis XIV or Napoleon? Too few things for us to spend much time occupying ourselves with them; worse, I see that our traditions sometimes occult the horizons to come from our eyes. The abrupt bifurcation of the objects of our worries disrupts our past as well as the narratives that constituted our community. The gigantic size of these objects increases the size of our group by as much and lengthens the duration of the evolution that formed this group. The narrative now referred to by the new *we*, positively hominian, of the inhabitants of the planet, of the crew of the spaceship *Earth*, this narrative has quit the little stories of our narrow belongingnesses so as to recount the destiny of humanity over the entire space it has occupied; it's a matter of the Grand Narrative. As happens when we make a big turn on a journey, the landscape behind us reorganizes itself in its totality.

We no longer have the same objects; we no longer are the same subjects; we no longer form the same groups. Global-sized worries globalize the sizes of our collectives. We no longer run the same risks; we no longer maintain the same relations; we no longer inhabit different places; we haunt the same planet; we no longer live the same time. Who can claim that, while being subjected, on the shores of Brittany, to the cold winds issuing from a South American current, the breeze whose quivering is felt by one's eyebrow is limited to the landscape around one's house, to the quarter of one's city, to one's nation, even to one's continent? Who, while excavating today with his hands the process of being born and the decline of dying, the mutation of genes, the emergence, the eradication, the development of species, the long swings of the climate . . ., is comfortable breathing the length of a duration peculiar to eternal France, to the West, to Semito-Indo-European societies? We measure ourselves by the long time of plate tectonics and vital mutations. We no longer feel ourselves to have issued from the same time. We have changed spaces and durations.

We will not, I think, draw many lessons from history to help us pull out of this new pass. History concerns us less now than our prehistory, the evolution of living things, the time of the Earth and that of the Universe. We will now seek advice less from the annals recounted by Livy, Tocqueville or Marx than from the one counted by Lucy, Darwin and the Big Bang. Our foundational narratives have changed. The passionate interest in Rome, Washington or 'The Internationale' concerned those who wanted to dominate the Mediterranean or the world. The struggle for dominance will now no longer designate a distinguished group, a victor over others but will instead concern the conflictual relationships we all maintain with the world. Without realizing it, we have never ceased waging war against it. With what type of natural contract are we to end such a hidden conflict?

Wishes: in order to better understand and be able to act, let the institutes of political science merge as fast as possible with the institutes of the physics of the globe and the institutes of natural history; let the future decision-makers learn from this union how those for whom, tomorrow, they will bear societal responsibility will be born, will die, will be fed, will inhabit, will breathe, will work or not, will communicate and will even love; let them abandon their legends of the centuries in order to learn what million-year-old times the future is grafted onto.[8] Ignorance of the vast temporal flow that is traversing and immersing us today would hurl politics and administration into a dangerous desuetude.

What temporal flow? Look at certain rivers: they had, in the past, initiated a meander; suddenly, they abandoned it, like a forgotten arm, in order to run directly between both sides of its pocket, from an upstream site to a downstream side, while letting this between curve dry up. Thus, abandoning the old narratives to folklore, the new humanism's narrative directly links the adventure of hominization to the hominescent process that will manage the new world-objects. The course of the global Grand Narrative deserts the detour of history. The new *we* abandons the old divisions, borders, languages, states, nations, cultures, civilizations – dry. We fuse prehistory to the future. Our histories had forgotten the course of hominization; we have just, together, begun such a turn that we are taking this course up again. What human will be born from this? Humanity is becoming our project again: one that's not in any way abstract, not in any way formal or ideal, but risky, urgent, concrete, destinal; neither metaphysical nor moral: vital.

History's narratives are thus crushed between the autobiographies of singular subjects and the global Grand Narrative, which will recount, tomorrow, how the new community was formed in the face of the new objects. The Grand Narrative engendered, in the past, and the new narrative has forgotten and exceeded, since this morning, the prodigious bushiness of particular narratives, our old histories of France, Andorra or Eurasia, whose memories, if they remain, will at least be useful for lamenting, in return, the archaic cruelties and sublimities of the divisions, whose mosaic these

---

[8]Legends of the centuries = *légendes des siècles*. *La Légende des siècles* is the title of a collection of poems by Victor Hugo, which depicts the history of humanity.

histories established or confirmed, between languages, civilizations, spaces and human times. Let's measure the sufferings, the Evil and the beauties engendered by these divisions – the unfortunate magnificence of history. With what cost of blood have we paid for its rare cultural wonders?

The transformation of the subject into object

I shall go back to my beginning: the strength and detestation of rivals intensified the pleasant sensation of belonging; the more two heroes or groups dealt blows to each other, the better we recited their gest in order to feel ourselves together, delightfully. Execrable enemies are necessary to forge a subset. Suffer, die! This evil that is violence is always useful for something, at least for the collective fusion. As you can see, the army makes war, but in secret, better yet, war makes the army. When did the French nation begin? With the cry: *la Patrie en danger* [the country is in danger]! Everyone rallied to the borders. However, these exclusions that killed so many people can make a virtue of necessity. When a leak opens up in the ship's hull, the crew stops squabbling in order to run to the collision mats or pumps. The more the risk increases, the more unity is formed. So Evil no longer presents itself as a problem, but as a solution.

This is the new negative at work. The false god of groups needs the devil. Say, now, the name of this devil: he has changed it, as well as his status. For the new objects, with their vast shadow, worry us diabolically. They seem to us full of perils. Does this enemy threaten us? Do we have premonitions of catastrophes? So much the better! The more we feel the imminent danger, the faster we will abandon the morose delight in our histories so as to unite with one another in a new way. What a new thing, these enemies no longer have the name of humans.

Must we really free ourselves from fear and our enemies? No, don't free us from this entirely new evil; from it, peace can come, the greatest of all goods. Yes, the enemy changes status. From yesteryear up until yesterday, our histories had named him, accused him so that we would want to kill him. Of course, the scapegoat, the enemy who had come to cut the throats of our women, was ceaselessly reborn with each generation; history had to be rewritten. Bearing a proper name, this other advanced upon us in numbers, with heads high, dressed, helmeted, armed, like us. These rivals resembled us like brothers; twins killed one another in our battles. I am describing the conflict of slave against slave and sons against sons.

We have just changed these enemy subjects into objects of anxiety. We have transformed subjects into objects. A vast benefit! We will no longer fight against anything but the effects of our projects. Against the warming of the planet, against the deterioration of the climate, against the eradication of species, against the possible abuses of eugenics. . . . Our scapegoats have become ideas, programmes, technologies, tools, even better, world-objects. What post-historical luck!

We all more or less feel ourselves to be responsible for the dangers we are risking in the face of these things: will we no longer fight against anyone but ourselves? Behind the adversaries, the very people fighting them see the outlines of their own faces. Will we no longer kill anyone? We have found a new Other: no longer ourselves elsewhere, beyond our borders, but ourselves, together, projected tomorrow.

Everyone: world-we.

EVERYONE

OBJECTIVE AND COGNITIVE NARRATIVES

I have praised narrative – above even concepts – without defining it yet. Two elements are mixed in it: a relatively held-to line, whose continuity gathers random, contingent, chaotic grains. On the one side, format, on the other, bifurcations; so said *Branches*. In that book, there were two examples.

Ego: my life, my identity, my fate . . . proceed from a narrative that's multiple, variable, tiger-striped, gradated, coloured . . . that I hold, more or less, with myself and that I would hold with others if necessary. Whatever faithfulness or lie this narrative may recount, I will always find enough details in my own consciousness to verify it. No one can falsify this narrative. As for my consciousness, it has depended, from its emergence, on a musical voice that's sustained, temporary, broken, continuous, one which more or less organizes the granular background noise of the inward chaos. If I let the number and variety of the grains increase, I will have many things to recount, but will I dispose of a good channel for doing so? Conversely, I can tell informationless platitudes that everyone and I can understand.

We: the life, the fate of a group, belonging to a culture or a civilization . . . depend, in their turn, on a mythic narrative, on a history to which an ideology – whether false or true, sensible or deceitful – lends a meaning. However differently this thread may present itself, enough pertinent details are always found in the enormous chaos of past events to favour, clarify or even prove the coherence of its meaning. No one can falsify this meaning. Event-orientated history cites lots of information that is poorly enough retained; a history with finality can be divided up wonderfully but doesn't say more than the redundancy of the ideology that prescribes this end.

Homo sapiens: the Grand Narrative, for its part, recently found a temporal linking while preserving the contingency of its events. Let us seek what makes its newness.

So the formation of a narrative testifies to the incessant tension between the necessity to use pre-established forms, a format, in order to be able to communicate reliably and an equivalent obligation to break, to remake these forms because contingent circumstances end up restricting them and because pure and simple repetition wouldn't include any message.

In other words, the higher the probability of the occurrence of an element in a given situation, the less information this situation contains. Redundancy smooths and facilitates the channel; rarity fills it with content. Information grows in proportion to this rarity. Contingent circumstances weave, through their improbable newness, the text or content of the message, whereas repetition, connection, order, redundancy, format . . . facilitate the channel through which the message passes. No one hears anything but the unexpected, therefore the message, never the channel; or, conversely, we only hear what we expect, we only receive the channel, never the message.

Distinguished to the point of opposition, this hubbub of tatters and this redundant line, chance and necessity, follow the contours of our way of living time. I reminded above that one of the Greek roots of this word, *teinō*, *τείνω*, which signifies to stretch out, to elongate continuously, like the long flow of a paste or a fluid, contradicts the other possible root, *temno*, *τέμνω*, which signifies cutting up into small pieces, quasi atomic, as when duration is measured in centuries, minutes or microseconds. The same contradiction sculpts the word 'rhythm', flowing and broken. In fact, we experience the following as a continuous and unicursal flow: the hour of joy or of work, the day of rest or of pain, the life I claim to be mine, a history we feel to be ours . . ., but we also experience them as a distribution of dispersed segments, scattered intuitions, chances, misfortunes, hatreds, loves, waitings, despairs, incomprehensions, clarities . . .

The mixture evoked by the words derived from *temps* [time], like 'temperance', unite, like narrative, opposite elements, dry and mild, wet and cold, for 'temperature' and 'tempest'; benevolence and hardness of heart, practical wisdom and self-interest, for 'temperament'. . . . This mixture forms the *temps* of chronology as well as that of meteorology,[1] of the storms [*intempéries*] of love or the intermittencies of the intellect, so that it quite simply unites both of the aforementioned Greek roots: the continuous extension that can pass as the channel and the divided up grains that say the information. Time and narrative have the same components.

Thus, in its greatest generality, narrative is constructed like human duration, both subjective and collective, and like the time of the world. It is scientific and literary, cognitive and objective. The two laws that govern it, the chaos of random grains and the necessary continuity of a line, join up with the laws that found the very nature of time, in which, as I shall again forcefully emphasize, time [*le temps qui passe*] doesn't differ from the weather [*le temps qu'il fait*], in which, as I shall stress as many times as needed, physical time is composed as contradictorily as human time.

---

[1]Again, the word *temps* can mean either time or weather. To prevent confusion, the French often say *le temps qui passe* for time and *le temps qu'il fait* for weather, as in the following paragraph.

The narrative of Genesis and the narrative of genes

Talking about narratives without recounting is worth nothing. To do this, I am going to turn to one of the first narratives of my collective culture, which, more for the worse than for the better, occasionally enters into competition with the Grand Narrative.

But before Genesis was written, told or transmitted, before every narrative of history, one of the very first narratives propagated life itself; written, coded in four letters, whose combinations are repeated thousands of times, the genetic patrimony is duplicated and renewed by sexual mixture and mutations. Thus, it jumps from body to body and, in being transmitted, transforms them. Beginning with the most elementary organisms, messages pass and bifurcate, producing, through their format, their information and the accidents of epigenesis, the contingent double narrative of species in evolution and individuals in development. Already, in the secret recesses of the flesh, these fragments, which we are deciphering, of the Grand Narrative are being recounted.

Yet, gradually, certain genuses, having evolved, were no longer content with this genital transmission but imitated the gestures of their neighbours. Over a few million years, these animals extricated themselves from the long lineages of genetic automatons. A certain learning invaded the zone of instinct. At the end of a thousand children, the most mimetic of all animals began to propagate messages in a different way than by sex and bodies. By gestures, moans, cries, music, words, writings, telecommunications . . ., humans receive information from other people than their parents and broadcast it towards other people than their children. We interrupt and generalize genealogy through these signs, both carnate and disincarnate, circulating along adoptive and free exo-Darwinian paths. Hence newnesses of another order, which will never cease.

The varieties of format

Noises and songs, flying words, more stable writings . . ., these are our messages and narratives outside the body. To broadcast, to transmit and receive information, we obey, often without realizing it, numerous laws. Physical, sensorial and formal rules implacably reign over these propagations. For example: I don't beckon at night, I can't cry out in water, I don't gesticulate alone in my room, I don't speak Chinese at the Sorbonne, I don't mix my words any old how or write in dark ink on black paper. Acting like this, I will never receive your news. Our communications are first and foremost subject to as many formats. These latter go without saying.

It's a question of conditions without which nothing can be communicated. You wouldn't be able to read this book without the whiteness of the page, the equal size of the letters, without margins or pagination, alignments or paragraphs, without my respecting the spelling of my language, without my obeying the rules of its grammar, without my giving, broadly, the same meaning to words as you give to them, without the light of the sun or of your lamp, without a similar glow bathing the time and place of my writing, without our having, both of us, our sighted eyes, without a good teacher having taught us to write and read. . . . Necessary and multiple, these conditions format the message. Certain conditions concern inanimate matter: sun and paper, cutting and printing hardware; other conditions concern the living body: gaze and colours; lastly, other ones concern what I shall call software: signs and meanings, order and layout. All this only concerns the printed work. A similar multi-layered format regulates the messages transmitted and carried by DNA itself, by semaphores, gestural signs, calls and plaints, quartets or operas, recited poems or bad-mouthing rumours, by the telephone, the television, conventional or electronic mail. . . . In each of these instances, multiple formats govern at once the hardware recording medium, the sensory channel and the selected software. This innumerable whole is not seen, is not perceived at the moment of communication, but communication evaporates if it is lacking. Better yet, communication evaporates if it isn't repeated, if it isn't sustained, if it doesn't remain constant over the duration of the conversation or exchange, over the time of the narrative. The most important part of the format – I am using the singular to express this innumerable whole, this triple family of rules – lies in its constancy and its repetition. This is why it stays transparent: it doesn't contain any information. Conversely, information is defined as what isn't repeated.

Therefore, this channel-format, repeated the whole time, obeys the principle of identity. It resembles logic, mathematics, eternity. Leibniz said that the eternal truths were deduced from the principle of identity, as though they did nothing but repeat it; they participate, he claimed, in God's understanding, the understanding of He who said: I am what I am, a redundant subject or a redundancy of the subject. This resaid identity characterizes this format and the form of the subject, eternity as well as necessity. Without this resaid identity, nothing can be said, but it alone says nothing.

As you will recall, when I was recounting my autobiography, that originarily synthetic unity, me identical to me, remained stable and identical amid the granular chaos of time and noise. If I recite, likewise, some history, it will have to do, for example, with the Eternal City, the forever-existing Rome. The narrative's subject is repeated almost as much as the format. Narrative thus shows a stable form, a stable identity, *I* or *we*, close to the format, like a layer adhering to the channel, which flows then, even more fluidly.

The performative format: Narrative of origin or origin of narrative?

I hardly dare to touch upon the first words of Genesis, objects of faith, texts commented on, debated, venerated, ridiculed thousands of times. Nevertheless, here they are. The great week of Creation begins with the sentence *in a beginning in which God created the heavens and the earth*, and ends with *such was the birth of the heavens and the earth*. These two quasi-repetitions, between which God announced himself and withdrew and in which the world came into existence, open and close, with their redundancy, the box that contains the message and whose envelope is formed by these two repetitions.

Quasi musical in its rhythm, the message, for its part, cadences the repetition of the seven days. There was an evening, there was a morning, on the *nth* day; it suffices to vary on the count of the days. Quasi musical in its rhythm, the message cadences the power of the performative word. God said *let something be*, and something was. It suffices to vary on the days; it suffices to vary on the things. Quasi musical in its rhythm, the message cadences separation. God separated the lower waters from the upper waters, the sea from land, day from night. It suffices to vary on the things separated, on the things and the days. Quasi musical in its rhythm, the message cadences naming. God called the firmament heavens, the continent earth and the gathered together waters sea. It suffices to vary on the things separated, to vary on the things named. Quasi musical in its rhythm, the message cadences the enjoyment of the Creator. God saw that this, God saw that that – it suffices to vary – that everything he had made, in sum, was good. Amid the regularity of these rhythms, one hardly notices a slight quantitative progression between the works of the days, as though their *tempo* was increasing, an augmentation due to the multiplicity of the things produced, rare at the beginning, like the heavens and earth, but increasingly powerful when the stars are lit and the living things swarm about.

A ritornello of time, of production by speech, of the disjointed, of the called, of the satisfied, I hardly dare to say that rhythm wins out over variation, harmony over song, repetition over the things varied, that the redundancy of the message, a maximal redundancy, tends, in the end, towards identity. Would a day be enough to say and make everything? I hardly dare to write that at the end of the third day, at the rate the saying and things were going, the probability that the same words would return strongly tended towards certainty. Yet when this probability increases, the information content decreases proportionately and to the point of being nullified. Might I dare to write that the performative wins out over information? Quickly, when Saturday arrives, the message risks no longer saying anything at all. Here is rest. The lesson: in the reign of redundancy, of identity, of the performative, in the kingdom of Eternity, in the insistency of the format and of the subject, the perfection of the channel annihilates the abundance of information. Optimal saying makes everything but doesn't say anything. Doesn't say anything but the all-powerfulness of saying.

I have told about the music and rapped out the rhythm. I am going back, to justify them, to before the beginning, to before the box that contained this cadenced message in its envelopes was opened and closed. Surprise for the creation said to be *ex nihilo*, there is a state preceding this beginning, a state in which the desert, darkness, abyss and the unformed mass of the primordial waters reign, in which hubbub dominates. The noise met with in my soul and my group has returned. A flat and formatted rhythm, a smooth plain, on the one hand, which protects us like a wall from this background noise made, on the other hand, by the waves of the sea, by the fundamental brouhaha of the countless multiplicities that no music, that no speech has yet measured, the gasping behind the silence. The granulous, then the unified. The multiple and the one. The diverse and the homogeneous. The crackling and the monotonous. The roaring irrational chaos and the Being that is, redundant. The unsayable and the repetitive. Rhythm follows the varied. The week details the pre-existent of the Sunday before: the Single and the noise. Two times or temporalities: identity, alterity; format and bifurcations; chance and necessity.

That it takes the regular rhythm of music to plane down the disordered detail of multiplicities, to smooth out their deafening buzzing, is, in fact, a lesson given to us by the world and its elements (seas, volcanoes, earthquakes and winds), by the singularities or the various species of the living, but that was also given to us by my consciousness of myself, at the outermost bounds of carnal heat, given to us again by the anonymous crowds in which we became lost, as well as by the nations that threw us into wars howling with hatred, the lesson of the subjective, the collective, the objective, but of the cognitive too, the lesson of consciousness, of history, of the universe and of knowledge, the chief lesson given to us here by God. The double-entry lesson of every possible narrative.

So Genesis's narrative begins here. Narrative's genesis begins here as well. I speak, we speak, they speak, in sum He speaks. Immediately, this speech performs, separates, calls and enjoys. It repeats, identitary, and cuts every multiplicity short. It cuts so short that it brings to a sudden end. Disorder withdraws and can no longer withstand it. In return, disorder doesn't nourish the speech with any content. God says: I am what I am; I speak and I create what is. Everything comes to an end in a repeated word. There is no narrative. The genesis of narrative begins with such a small narrative that it nullifies the narrative; the very first law of this narrative, the eternal principle of identity, annihilates, with repetitions, time and every possible narrative. Barely shorter than a small cadenced week.

So, for the true, the genuine, the developable, the temporal narrative to begin, it must truly be opened up to what interrupts identity, to what breaks redundancy, to the chaotic multiplicity, to the brouhaha, to the hubbub. In the first beginning, God speaks; he never stops saying; the word does nothing but talk. In the second beginning, He is going to talk a little, then no longer talk much, then withdraw into a transcendent absence. So the other Grand Narrative begins. Enter man and woman. They are no longer going to stop talking so as to fill up, in detail, the vast silence of God. Enter alterity, disorder, the rarity of singularities.

Numbers

When we begin a narrative, whether oral, written, by signs or electronically, we first make sure, as I said, of the format. Of the light, the white page, the black ink, visibility, hearing and orthographic, semantic, syntactic . . . correctness. We certainly don't go back over, each time, the alphabet of letters, the sol-fa of notes, the sequence of numbers or the table of atoms; we consider them, virtually, to be acquired. But everything happens as though we could, from time to time, verify their presence, their faithfulness. For without them, the narrative would vanish.

In this regard, the number series can serve as an image. Among the numbers, the prime numbers produce the others, which only repeat combinations of them. Unlike the alphabet, the sol-fa or the table of elements, their sequence, infinite, is distributed strangely in the ordinal infinity of integers. At the beginning, there are a lot of them: five, from 1 to 10, four, from 11 to 20, and so on. We don't know the law of their appearance. But we do know that as the counting progresses, they become increasingly rare and unexpected to the point that we become surprised when we find them, like flecks of gold in the common muds of a torrent. The world resembles the prime numbers sown in the other numbers.

We are wandering in ordinary space when a place of beauty that makes the heart race suddenly appears. We are wandering in the time of history, the adventure of life, the anonymous crowd and, all of a sudden, an exceptional moment, a delightful chance and an opportune encounter seize, with their thunderbolt, the intelligent intuition, the vague womb or the soul and transport to seventh heaven. The world, duration and mass are sown with gold flecks, rare summits, dense instants or first women.

The Bible recites God the way I count the numbers. At the beginning, in the seven first days, the Creator is repeated; present, only He is seen, only He is heard; everything is produced from His speech. After the week, he enters his rest. He will talk again, but not much, much less, less and less; his speech is going to become increasingly rare and unexpected, up to the point that we become surprised, crying miracle, when someone recognizes Him, here and now, like a fleck of gold in the common and cruel multiplicities of history, like the punctual tangency of transcendence over the confused waters of immanence, like constancy in forgetfulness, like verification of the format amid the vast abundance of transmitted things. At the beginning of the world and the narrative, the eternal principle of identity repeats its format so much that the message loses all information. Certainty is overflowing, rarity is lacking.

The first woman

Then history begins, then begins the narrative – in which speech still tries to play its performative role. God creates the man in His image and His resemblance, and Adam will name the garden's plants and animals the way the Creator named night and day. If this were to continue, there would never be any narrative, never be any information; there would only be identity, due to lack of rarity.

Happily, the woman came about. She thwarted the performative of the divine word. Both order and omnipotence are characterized by the circumstance that a fact immediately follows from the said by the very fact of saying it. God says: don't touch this fruit, and straightaway, tempted by some reptile, Eve consumes it. The first rarity, therefore the first information, breaks the principle of identity, namely, the fact that's identical to the said. The flaw in omnipotence, the disobedience to order, this is the true beginning of history. Narrative always begins with a bifurcation that breaks repetition. The mother of humanity, Eve bears the matrix of every possible narrative. History commences with the fall. The woman thwarts the principle of identity, puts information into redundancy, breaks the level ice of eternity and invents history by throwing rarity into repetition. Genesis's God plays the role of universal format; Eve, singular, breaks the format.

Starting from this, history displays a double rarity. First, the diversified abundance of human disobedience. The woman and the male, individuals and groups, are going to use their genius to make wild variations of all sorts of crimes. Killing one's brother, one's daughter, whoever, raping the wife of one's servant . . ., the narrative begins to abound with these rarities, increasingly common, to the point of falling back into monotony. During the time of this narrative, God, absent, appears, sometimes, rarely, speaks to the prophets, the prophets speak for and about Him, shines forth at the summit of Sinai, sows his lack into history. Redundant in the past, he is now extremely rare in the narrative. While sin, rare at first, then frequent, passes from information to redundancy, God, conversely, passes from repeated identity to rare appearance.

History, but also every narrative in general, combines two laws: the one and the multiple; the same, repeated, with the other, diversified; redundancy and unexpected rarity; stable format and bifurcations; Eve simply bifurcates on the performative's redundant format. But, in addition, the Bible makes two laws, divine and human, intersect. The one God, the Creator, plays the role of format and retains eternity. Diverse and non-performative, human speech enters into time, which is unpredictable like human speech and its speakers. But the biblical narrative makes the two roles intersect, in image and counterimage. The disobedient and sinful bifurcation is overabundant, to the point that it lapses into repetition, plunging human history into the redundant monotony of crime. Cram packed with information, the narrative, little by little, loses information. So, begun in the unpredictable, history enters into repetition. Conversely, divine identity, begun in performative and creative redundancy, moves, little by little, into rest, withdraws, goes lacking, becomes increasingly absent and makes itself so rare and so unpredictable that it passes, for its part, from nullity of information to fullness of information.

Does a narrative exist as crammed packed with information as the one that shows the highest rarity? Thus, switching around the two laws, two histories intersect: the history of human multiplicities and the history of divine unity, the history of a disobedience that's so frequent that it turns into habit and the history of an eternity that's so rarely present that it turns into event. The narrative only recounts crimes, to the point of no longer saying anything but their high probability, the certainty that violence will ravage us all the way up to Hiroshima; at the same time, the narrative only recounts absence, waiting, the hope for the rarest chance, recounts the most heart-rending of our lacks, to the point of persuading us of its improbability. Consequently, there is nothing certain except Evil; there is no newness without hope except the Messiah, whose coming, endlessly delayed, will deliver us. So, can the maximum or optimum of information redeem its loss? Does hope redeem all our certainties? Equipped with these two intersected laws, does this narrative contain the matrix of every possible narrative?

Evil, the first matrix

Since literature is born with Evil, I don't need transgression in order to understand this Evil. For a narrative only begins by breaking with identity, by putting an obstacle in front of performative speech, by bifurcating on repetition. Without this bifurcation, this obstacle, this rupture, redundancy would prevent a narrative from beginning by emptying the message of all information content. Before the woman, there were only repeated images or similitudes. God created the man according to his likeness the way he had created the world according to his speech. A reduced model of this paradise-world, Eden was filled with named plants. The woman refused repetition. She sinned by forgetting Being. The fall broke the redundancy. The disobedience split with identity. The sin inclined the parallelism of the images. Every possible narrative begins at the exit from the performative paradise when an inclination breaks open the bifurcation of time. Eve invents literature. One could talk passionately about sin, wrongdoing, transgression, radical evil, about the devil and all that goes with him, but everything reduces, with a marvellous simplicity, to the inflecting of identity, to an angle on redundancy, to a slippery slope quitting the uniform plain of the performative. Eve opens up the angle that causes time to be born starting from eternity and causes multiple and circumstantial, singular and varied speech to be born starting from a sustained monotony. Of the devil, I only see his forked cloven foot.

Certain people dreamed of enjoying the performative. Jurists succeeded in this and discovered in law places, times and circumstances in which saying 'the session is open' would in fact open the session and in which pronouncing a sentence of death caused, ipso facto, a head to be chopped off. Said or written, the law has the force of law. The legislator, semi-divine, reflects the image of God the legislator. But, outside of law, the dream quickly lapses into nightmare. King Midas received, it is said, the ability to turn everything he touched into gold, as though his skin was endowed with the power of the philosopher's stone. He desired gold, he had gold, but, out of redundancy, everything became gold. When he was hungry or thirsty, the bread he broke, the wine he poured, the salt he sprinkled immediately changed into nuggets and ingots, leaving him to die of hunger. There, the performative of wealth; here, the performative of desire: whatever Sade desired, the divine marquis desired, in addition, that the person he desired desire it like he did. This height of aristocratic arrogance ended in murderous monotony. What could be more redundant than sadistic crimes if not the reigns of tyrants athirst, as well, for a performative power? Dionysius of Syracuse, Emperor Caracalla, Louis XIV (the bewigged precursor to Stalin) or the vile Pol Pot – the same deadly uniformity.[2] Others, lastly, desired the performative of reason and found it in dogma, in the infallibility of absolute knowledge: a shipwreck into inflexible stupidity. In every one of these instances, gold or sex, power or truth, the performative turns into the death of people or of the intelligence. Empty of information, redundancy throws into nothingness, amid the monotonous count of the *colonnes de Buren*. In wanting to imitate this idea of God, we transform into poor sterile or dangerous devils, without history or narrative, except for the count of the graves in the cemeteries.

A tremendous subject in the matter of beginnings, God dissolves his omnipotence into weakness, extinguishes his word into muteness. He begins his Passion. His dense presence evaporates into a virtual form such that everyone can disobey him, freely. And only evoke him, invoke him, sing of him by signs that can scarcely be written or said. So vanished that almost no indication of him exists. The multiple noise of the historical uproar covers over the unicity of the performative word. Worse, should this word reappear,

[2]For the first in the list, Serres wrote Diodorus. Since Diodorus was a historian and not a tyrant, I presume that he meant Dionysius of Syracuse.

in flesh and blood, an event that's so improbable and rare that no one would be able to believe in such a quantity of information, everyone would set upon him to the point that he would die. The subject that's the size of the world becomes an object the size of nothingness.

But the cries of the din of history only clamour about him. Yes, this cultural hubbub designates thousands upon thousands of diverse objects, but all of them bear this lack, this hole of the absent virtual. Lost, the subject becomes the lost object. To be found again, to be rediscovered passionately. The infinitely powerful subject of every beginning, God becomes the infinitely weak and unperceived objective of the end.

The unfolding of a continuous spectrum across distinct variations

A reprisal of the theme and of the first variation: Speech

So history resounds with divine absence, barring one exception: when such silence falls, psalmists sing or prophets rant and rave. The more of His necessity there is, the less information there is, which, conversely, grows with the chance that is disobedience. The more necessity there is, the less narrative there is, which abounds the more it pours into contingency, when god withdraws. The Big Bang of the Bible-bomb: from identity to alterity, from repetition to contingency, when the narrative begins, history explodes, *ex nihilo*. Dense with information, history shoots up from an ahistorical week, with zero information. Chance shoots up from necessity. Everything is reversed starting from Eve.

I sometimes think that she opened up a crack in the smooth wall that was built so that the identical, with its order, would protect us from the hubbub. Due to her, noise wells up within the redundant silence.

The birth of time: there is no longer any eternal return. Time begins at the contingent tangency of eternity, where the identical and the repetitive rule; its duration commences at the end of the ritornellos that order the creative week. Time is born from improbable disobedience, from the unbelievable loss, by the divine word, of its performative power, a throw of the dice, a chance that, by its rarity, causes the quantity of information to explode, therefore launching narrative time. The irreversibility of time ensues from this contingency, from this rarity, from this bifurcation, from the opening of the narrative; narrative doesn't so much unfold in time as time instead is defined by the profile, invented here, of narrative. Nullifying narrative would return to the reversible; returning to the reversible would nullify narrative. Time surges up from eternity, like chance from necessity.

The second variation: Atoms

At the farthest distance in relation to what has preceded, let's move from the Semitic zone to Greco-Latinity, from Jerusalem to Rome and Athens, from the spiritual to the material, from the religious to the scientific, from prose to poetry, from speech to atoms, from the soft to the hard, from God to the atheistic repudiation of the divine. As far removed as possible from the first variation, the beginning of the world said, drawn, calculated, sung and recited by Lucretius nevertheless unfolds the same model.

At the origin, a rain of atoms falls eternally, in parallel lines, in an unvarying emptiness. Repetitive and redundant, order reigns ab initio: the homogeneous regularity of an infinite and monotonous environment, a uniform motion, a laminar flow. Random, improbably distributed, at uncertain times and places, in the smooth extension and smooth duration, the differential *clinamen*, infinitely small, suddenly breaks this identitary eternity of the fall of the elements in the white emptiness and favours, by the resulting vortex, the lashing together of things, the encounters of history, even the composition of words. Absurd, inconceivable, impossible even, tangent and contingent, its declivity blocks the vertical fall, the way disobedience contradicted the performative. A disorder is introduced into the prior order.

No narrative can ever recount the geometric parallelism, outside of time, of the elementary rain because it doesn't contain, due to its repetition, any information. Via the first circumstance, narrative begins – via this inclination, at random, in the fall of an atom, via the tangent to a beginnings of turbulence, via the contingency of time in the eternal. Let's decline this swerving declension in the feminine; conversely, I would like to say that Eve inclines and praise the matriarch of its turbulence. So, the entire universe of things, the history of humans and Lucretius's poem together shoot up from this vortexing throw of the dice. Atoms become entangled and things are born; codes intermingle and words appear. Thus narrative shoots up from silent eternity via a chance sown on necessity.

I sometimes think that the *clinamen* resulted from an abrupt tear in the smooth wall of emptiness, here built so that the identical, with its order, would protect us from the hubbub emitted by the world's background noise. Due to it, noise wells up within the fall's silence.

These narratives oppose each other while remaining twins: materialist, mechanist and atheist, this second model expresses the monotheistic, spiritual and linguistic creationism of the Bible in another language – there is no paradox in what I am saying. What the one draws, the other says; what the one schematizes with particles, the other recounts with speech; the eternal order traced by the one in parallel lines in space is placed by the other, as rhythm, in the performative of an all-powerful language; the hole of disorder opened up by turbulence here is torn open by disobedience there. All in all, quite heavy in differences, these variations nonetheless bring to light a dazzling isomorphism: in both instances, narrative, time, history, world, everything that exists and moves, plus everything that can be said about them, emerge from a lightning-fast short circuit that puts order and disorder, redundancy and bifurcation, the identical and the vortexing, chance and necessity into relation. At the exit from the mute whiteness, narrative shoots up from the improbable; at the borders of identity, information surges up from a rarity; at the tangency of the eternal, time comes out of the contingent. An invariant across variations establishes a connection between the two models beyond their divergences. Do they translate, each from their side, a schema that may be inevitable or difficult to get beyond, in which, in a way, chance would mix with necessity?

The third variation: Physics

The invention, during the Renaissance and maybe starting from the Middle Ages, of modern science consisted in the application of mathematics to physical experiments, in the encounter of an identitary language possessed of universal principles, on the one hand, and the multiple and irreducible singularities of the real, on the other; that is, in the originality of a new tangency between two worlds, that of chance, that of necessity.

Why did this discovery arise so late when the Greeks of antiquity had everything they needed, it seems, to attain it? They couldn't invent it because they believed in necessity. The birth of geometry made a flash of brilliance that dazzled and blinded their thought – with good reason. The sudden emergence of the necessary in things and words fills anyone who reflects with wonder. Many among the Greeks believed that it sufficed to trust in this divine mastery to understand everything: politics and humanity, music and the world, all the way down to the detail of causes and reasons;

that it sufficed to deduce. Along these long, entirely simple and easy chains of reason, they came across a strangeness that we ourselves, perhaps, have not yet explained. By what miracle, Kant and Einstein exclaimed, for example, and as one voice, does some given theorem, formal and abstract, apply to some given concrete circumstance of things? By what mystery does this circumstance here touch the universality of that statement there; in brief, is this chance tangent to this necessity?

For a moment, Plato believed that, aided by the Demiurge, his *Timaeus* could deduce the detail of the world from mathematics and that, like the atoms of matter, its triangles and polyhedrons of form would, of themselves, compose the four inanimate elements, the universe and the living things. He fell flat, for he was mistaken. This fall reverberated for a long time, and we had to wait at least until the Renaissance to get back up from it again.

If Plato definitely believed in such a miracle, his Demiurge, however, had the initial intelligence to construct his astronomy by intersecting the circle of the Same with that of the Other so as to open, in this way, the oblique angle of the ecliptic. Surprise, again: eternitary and redundant, identity encounters, at the vernal point of springtime, a strange alterity that contradicts it, so that the narrative of the universe could commence or become possible. Have I been saying anything else for some time now? Even within the formal project of only retaining the effectiveness of the mathematical Ideas or Forms, even inside the dream of universal deduction, an incredible and hollow dream that would cost the Greeks attaining modern science, inclination returned, introducing noise again into the redundancy of the Same so that the narrative of the beginnings of the world could open up.

One will not be surprised that Milton and so many others, later on, had recognized the trace of original sin and of Eve's fall in the inclination of the ecliptic, whose benevolence, nonetheless, produces the seasons and their fruits. However naive and laughable this translation may appear today, it has an abstract form that serves as the sole object of my thinking here. Eve resembles an Other even better than the author of *Paradise Lost* had dreamed. Everything is happening as though a rigorous model was traversing, with its stable structure, narratives of origin – or origins of narrative – that are the most different, the most opposed in appearance. In fact, in comparing Lucretius's *clinamen* with the inclination brought about by the Other on the Same in the Platonic heavens, one still wonders why the Friends of the Forms had engaged for so long in such a Picrocholine battle against the Sons of the Earth, and for what absurd reasons certain countries, said to be civilized, still rumble with it today.

And now, what did Galileo think and do at the end of the Renaissance? He read, he said, a world written in mathematical language. Of course, but the mystery returns here: Can we predict what sentence of this language will express, here or there, this or that phenomenon? Can we deduce, conversely, some given appearance from some given theorem? No, the world and its language reply with one voice. Neither the one nor the other allows this key to be discovered. This language alone does not allow predicting what region of the world will follow one of its prescriptions, nor does some given region of the world allow predicting what sentence of the language will say it. The interworld of forms doesn't descend, of itself and predictably, point by point, region by region, onto the world as it is, which, conversely, doesn't ascend, as it is and place by place, towards its language. Application isn't done all by itself, automatically, as it were. Experimentation is needed.

The inevitable character of experimentation comes from the fact that we cannot predict which theorem will be adapted, for example, to the falling of bodies. Can we say why, there, a quadratic equation imposes itself, whereas, here, for another region, we shall need to use an integral, or, for elsewhere, a tensor? Experiment alone suggests this, indicates this, dictates this. In other words, the world displays contingency with respect to the necessary language, which, nonetheless, best expresses it. Somehow or other, necessity is tangent to things that are random with respect to it. Thus, like a refrain, what I have been continually saying has returned.

As a result, this refrain extends so widely that modern science is defined by this bifurcation, this inadequate knot, this intersection of the Same and the Other, this encounter of necessity with chance, this fragility of adaptation, this narrative principle. . . . Mechanics, astro- or geophysics, thermodynamics, biochemistry . . . are forever applying necessary laws, mathematically formulated, to regions of the world, to singularities of time, of space, of motions, of forces. Name a single science that would do without this tension between a logically coherent guiding thread and a thousand splintered grains of things forming a contingent landscape, without a tangency of the former, mathematical, to the latter, experimental. Globally necessary, methodically required, the fact remains that this correspondence enters, for local detail, into the unpredictable; no one can say, before all experimentation, what equation, what inequality, what formula will come out of it. Therefore we shall define application as a bringing into relation, as a contingent tangency between chance and necessity.

The fact that the Grand Narrative now recounts the global whole of these bringings into relation will only surprise those who don't understand that modern science, on the very morning of its emergence, was already, in this way, taking on the form of a narrative.

Furthermore, and we have only become aware of this recently, the only decisive experiment remains the one that falsifies laws that are in force, which once again are redundant in the preceding model. One more verification teaches nothing, owing precisely to its repetition, whereas experiencing a failure launches a bifurcation, another possibility. So information increases, and the narrative sets off again. Many scientific inventions have proceeded from an experiment that resolutely set about by refusing to say the predicted, interrupting redundancy. Long live error and falsity! So the history of science can be told as an unpredictable series of world views that topple because of missed appointments. At the very heart of the sciences of precision and exactness, we find, as in every other narrative, rupture of law, disobedience to the rule, that which puts a grain or a thorn in a level channel. Without this falsity, the history of true science would not even have begun. It would, moreover, never have rebounded.

Falsification continually opens up a second song in the advance of science, the way Eve's disobedience opened up the second chapter of Genesis. And, despite the distance between these two cultural regions, for similar reasons. A falsifying experiment, in the narrative of knowledge, plays a role that's isomorphic to the one played, in the paradise-garden, by the sudden appearance of Evil, of misfortune, of accident, of the fall or, rather, of inclination in the fall. Contingency takes on a thousand masks: here, of the false, there, of Evil, elsewhere, of the improbable . . ., all in all, of disobedience. Many Eves haunt our laboratories; a significant percentage of Nobel Prize winners, crowned with laurels when old, suffered in their youth from projects rejected by ad hoc committees presided over by redundant gods who reasoned correctly. Does the history of science replay holy history? We sweat, suffer, die; mistaken, we make mistakes, are wrong and discover, surprised but cheerful, that those who always claim to be right stammer out their redundancy.

If you repeat, in research, what teaching has taught you, you will have an honourable career in the university, where citations are respected, that is to say, copying the Same. If, on the contrary, you bifurcate, you risk experiencing the fate of Mendel, Semmelweis or Boltzmann, brilliant precursors, misunderstood and persecuted, driven into the shadows or to suicide. The next generation will venerate you, dead, as prophetic and revolutionary. Even with inventions, the victim becomes, after his death and banishment, a god by apotheosis.

To finish, I would like to rectify one of Galileo's sayings. He judged the world to be written in mathematical language. This intuition inaugurated modern science. Philosophers and scientists have never reconsidered this formula since they have never stopped penning, successfully as we know, this language. I practice it as well, admire and honour it. But I now believe that mathematics expresses the format of the world. Mathematics doesn't so much say its language as describe its format. The world speaks, it even writes, of course, sometimes better than we do, more exactly and faithfully than we do – since the Grand Narrative, exact, reads this writing – but, in any case, not like we do, who speak in languages, who write in no matter what conventional letters, notes, sounds or elements and construct languages. The world gives a format. The given is given in a format; the constructed is written or spoken. Nature is formatted; culture is said or written. Thus, our mathematics say, express, write, describe, clarify, present, analyze, show, prove the world's format.

More generally, what we call the subject seems to me to merge into the format. I establish the format of my autobiography, of what I and others recount about me; the format, not the governor. The *we* likewise establishes the format of our histories, and not their government; the world and humanity lastly establish the format of the Grand Narrative and not its governing rudder. Whether mystery or transparency, does God establish the Universe's format?

The fourth variation: Life

I shall attempt to recount, as at the beginning of this chapter, the evolutionary narrative of the living. It was raining elements and letters, as I have recently said, speaking of antiquity. For today's knowledge, simple atoms and compound molecules were striking and colliding with each other for billions of years, according to repetitive laws, those of heat, entropy or cooling, those of gravity, attraction or repulsion, and others still, iterated identically in all the universe. The alphabet of the simple bodies and the alphabet of these compounds, of a marvellous simplicity, can be repeated as much as you please. So it was raining letters, for us, chemists, the way it had been raining atoms, in Lucretius, a physicist. Suddenly, four amino acids appeared, a certain combination of which possessed a strange faculty, that of self-replication.

The event does not reside in that, for nothing has changed yet, since, local here, as well as global for physical laws, replication repeats the reign of the Same. While the laws of the inanimate were continuing to occupy the global universe with their redundancies, a new narrative, biochemical for its part, began locally from the first translation error, from the moment repetition made a mistake, from the first slip, from the first mutation, which thus played the role of another inclination, one as improbable, as random, as minuscule as it was, but erroneous, but disobedient, but falsifying, but monstrous, a hopeful monster. So mutation, here and there, at uncertain times and places, continually launches disorderly recombinations, although often economical, from which evolution and development ensue, an evolution and development in which individuals and species are born, change and disappear in a narrative that endlessly tries, in unfolding them, as many recombinations, which are invented by these mutating bifurcations.

On the other hand, present and active, selective pressure cuts and carves into these inventions, filters them through the necessary iteration of death; repetitive, redundant, tragically performative, selective law has nothing more to say than these monotonous slaughters. Jacques Monod said: chance is mixed with necessity. Unpredictable, contingent, deadly, living things incarnate and prepare the contingency of history, which is as deadly and as unpredictable as they are. Recount biochemistry like a narrative; relate biochemistry like life; recite biochemistry like time.

Again, without any paradox, here are four isomorphic models: two ancient narratives, Genesis and Lucretius's physical one, and two more recent ones, a neo-Darwinian one and a Renaissance one, the latter stable and inanimate, the former evolutionary and living, that is, four narratives in which redundancy and contingency mix, in which chance causes narrative to shoot up starting from necessity. Eve contradicts the performative's rule; the *clinamen*'s obliquity blocks gravity's vertical law; falsification causes the norm to bifurcate; mutation betrays translation. Sin, absurdity, falsity, error. A hole opens up through which noise wells up; the whole of narratives commences. And what if we ranked Eve, our mother, among the hopeful monsters? The same law makes twins out of narratives that our debates set in opposition. Thus, varying four times on an unpredictably common theme, I invite you to laugh at battles that instead set people who understand poorly in opposition, enemy brothers, which one of the next variations shall talk about.

Communication: Temporary balance sheet

Just as much as inward narratives and collective histories, the hard sciences therefore deal with a necessary continuum as much as with a discontinuity of chance events. Sciences: Newton and Einstein on the one side, but *quanta* on the other. Narratives: a fated drama on the one side, but encountered circumstances on the other.

I have sensed this for half a century; communication and its constraints aid a synthesis between the pure and abstract logics, the experimental sciences and the general literature of cultural phenomena. I shall repeat this so as to facilitate my own message's channel: the flow's bed, the thread of every message – the universal system, the continuous line, the general abstract, the necessary . . . – impede their information content – the singular, the contingent, the detail of the concrete, the packets of *quanta*, the deafening grains of chaos, chance itself. . . . Taken up, managed, maintained in any case, this contradiction of two laws or of two universes (which are suitable for the work of language as well as for our experience of time), whose relationship, stretched, varies from one domain to the other, constructs the whole of what we communicate in language, with language and through language.

Through four variations on these two terms, I have begun to unfold an objective and cognitive spectrum, in the sense of the spectrum of colours, in which each coloured band is composed of one of these variations. Having departed, for the moment, from a narrative considered to be symbolic or even mythic, it continued on, paradoxically, through more established knowledge: physics, ancient or modern, biology. Via other variations or bands, I am going to push it, again, from the hardest logic to soft literary genres.

But I shall particularly conclude that, absolutely new, the Grand Narrative presents both the height of the necessary and the height of the contingent, both the optimum of the universal – every law of every science – and the maximum of singularities – every circumstance that comes about in the time of the universe and its minuscule tail of history.

Does the Grand Narrative thus bridge the global spectrum of messages, which separates logico-mathematical language from the contingent and chaotic circumstances of event-based narrative? Maybe, for its newness comes from the fact that in it, by an unexpected reversal characterizing the epistemology of our day, the most rigorous laws become, precisely, contingent circumstances. On a gigantic scale, its time unfolds a kind of arborescence in which, onto the exact laws of quantum mechanics, of relativity, of astrophysics, the laws, as exact, of general mechanics and of geophysics are grafted or connected, unexpectedly and unpredictably, onto which are grafted, contingently, the laws of biochemistry, just as precise, the laws of living species, from which humanity surged up . . ., each bifurcation causing new laws for a new time to arise. Thus, it presents a contingent bushing-out of connected necessities. I shall return to this.

Preparation for the fifth variation

But here, again, passed in review and summed up, is the announced spectrum. To draw it, I began by varying on one of the oldest narratives to have formed my culture. Globally, the Bible projects, as I have said, the universal design spoken by the divine word onto the details of the world, onto the freedom of individuals and that of a group, onto the contingency of their acts; monotheistic speech shapes events that most often resist its law: disobedient kings, people enamoured with idols. This projection, in which the two elements brought to light here unite and contradict one another, produces holy history.

As a singular example, the very beginning of Genesis, the object today of an absurd debate, is divided (I haven't said this) into two parts, which the learned claim, plausibly, draw on at least two distinct sources. The first one, stylistically cadenced, of cosmogonic significance, only allows the creator God to speak. Order reigns there; several divisions separate the heavens and the earth, light and darkness . . . and produce all things; the man and the woman take their places, at the week's end, in a logical harmony; repetitions, refrains or ritornellos, as though chanted, ensure a coherence and a perfect memorization there. Here is a rigour, laws – in short, what characterizes redundancy, the channel's format and necessity.

In the second part, on the contrary, God dictates little, save for forbidding or helping, whereas the serpent, woman and man, in their turn, speak; a hesitant, complex, interwoven style ends with an unpredictable act, the fruit of this contingent freedom that is going to become both the subject matter of and the obstacle to the difficult realizations of the divine design in human history. Why this need for two sources, since both principles of narrative mobilize its *incipit*?

Productive of history in the usual sense, as I am going to say, this prophetic narrative of judges and kings recounts, next, how transcendence, omnipotence, providence and their sovereign laws attempted to sculpt an immanence shot through with unruly insurrections. Issuing from the speech of the one God, this transhistorical project culminates in the Incarnation, in which, in a single person, divine and omnipotent eternity and human and mortal weakness coexist – contingency and necessity. Jesus Christ incarnates the hero of every narrative in his person.

The fifth variation: Histories

Substituted for this project of God, some meaning of history, dictated by some philosopher or other ideology, attempts, later and in its turn, to orient said events along the line of its thrust. The narratives of Condorcet, Hegel or the Marxists secularize those of the Bible, Pascal and Bossuet. The historian, I repeat, always finds, in the vast mass of occurred facts, enough events suitable for confirming his thesis. In all these histories (whether false or true, imaginary or probable is of no consequence), the most rational one as well as the most event-based, characters said to be providential – geniuses, saints, sublime heroes – appear and arouse the keenest interest, characters whose existence, devoted, incarnate the ideology in progress better than others. Varying but constant, the two elements of narrative return, sometimes carnally tied together in men and women, canonic in their turn. Consequently, I am repeating both my chapter on collective narratives and the first of my variations. The three variations that followed it pushed towards the hard sciences, on the side, quasi-divine, of necessity; now I am inclining it towards the soft sciences, more human, on the side of contingency.

Expelled from paradise, like Eve, the writing prophets of Israel therefore invented, after her, history such as we conceive and practice it; they no doubt led us into the idea that history only began with writing; without divine intervention, without the covenant contract between the Hebrew people and Yahweh, without the prophetic waiting for the Messiah, in brief, without intention and without finality, would we be able to hear, from the sequence of time, anything other than an incoherence full of noise, sound and fury, that only an idiot could tell? For a voice to be able to emit a narrative receivable by a human ear, for a time to unfurl, in brief, for history to exist, mustn't, on the one hand, a multiplicity of granular circumstances without order or coherence be, quite precisely, united in some way with some repetition, whose return would ensure the passing of the message, at least, its existence and its meaning, at most? The cries, the said, the written, the music of the Jewish prophets emit this returning call, this constancy, an invariance that injects order and a semblance of peace into the unheard-of disorder of misunderstandings and rivalries, violences and jealousies. From the depths of the ages, the West will never stop hearing, receiving and transmitting this teaching, this figure, this message, taken over by the Christian fulfilment. Granted, the West inherited *logos* from the Greeks, the word of proportion and measure, stemming from the figures of geometry, but it received from the Bible, in other figures, the speech that orders and that conceives time.

Outmoded, contemporary discussions regarding living things come from the difficulty we have in inventing a narrative other than the narrative of history, such as this latter was handed down to us by the prophets, in conceiving a purely contingent time, that is to say, stripped of an intention that would hold scattered elements together. The question boils down to this one: Can we think, yes or no, a repetition, a rule . . . without any finality, at bottom, without any anthropomorphism? The laws that rule over the Grand Narrative, the laws of mathematics, physics, biochemistry . . ., the whole of the reasonings I am using here, such as invariance across variations . . ., presuppose that in eliminating this difficulty, in therefore conceiving laws whose arrow, even if irreversible, is stripped of all intention, in conceiving formal rules without the anthropomorphism of a design, everything becomes of a limpid clarity and the battles become calmed in an admirable synthesis.

Those who see God as continually having the same design seem to me to be maligning His intelligence; this stubborn repetition, therefore without information, would instead designate a mediocre understanding. Predictable, an idiot keeps harping on about the same thing while refusing or planing down the unpredictable freshness whose awakening characterizes the sagacious person. Stupidity is characterized by a predictability whose redundancy brings it closer to the instinct of genetic automatons or the laws of gravity, whereas intuition spends, improbable, lavishly. If God exists and thinks or creates, I imagine – a victim of the same anthropomorphism as those I laugh at – I imagine, as I was saying, that, wildly intelligent, He loves to sow everything with the new and unexpected. What is to be thought from a redundant omniscience? What is to be hoped from a repetitive paradise? The wild proliferation of the contingent and unpredictable forms of living things bifurcating without warning on the proliferation, just as wild, in the universe, of inanimate forms, plus the proliferation, wilder still, of the improbable and contingent forms of innovative thought, this superabundant feast of sudden, unexpectedly arriving, disconcerting multiplicities engenders in me an elation and a plenitude that are so close to the divine that I have a tendency to project these attributes into him rather than leaving him with this old, stiff and stupid redundancy. The overflowing joy of intelligence shoots out from the omnitude of new things.

Let's return to time, marked with arrows for its part and invented by the Bible. Secularized, the laws people attempt to apply to history in order to give it a direction in fact do nothing but vary on the divine plan such as Bossuet, for example, took it up from the prophets, repeated it and translated it in his *Discourse on Universal History*. Individual or political, human actions are comprehensible, he said, if and only if the invisible hand of God moves them.

A scientist and theologian, Blaise Pascal rectified this idea by applying it to the progress of reason. When he described the generations as successively climbing onto the shoulders of the previous ones in order to see farther at each rung, he was translating the fulfilment of the divine plan into increasing human clarity. He gave progress to humans, whose labours were weaving a new Jacob's ladder.

This secularization would no longer stop, while leaving stable, beneath the different appearances, the plan's direction. The picture that Condorcet, already cited, painted of the progress of the human mind or spirit retranslates the biblical breath of inspiration into scientific discovery. Does the sequence of inventions in the sciences have a direction? Is it going somewhere? Can it be said to be endowed with intention? Do we invest it in human happiness? These questions still matter to us today. By working on time, by giving it a coherence and a direction, reason has taken over the reins, since the Enlightenment, from the creator God; reason has replaced the divine design described by the prophets. We have produced ourselves collectively.

That law of reason, variable, that reason calls class struggle or the invisible hand of the marketplace takes up again, on the left or the right, in Adam Smith or Marx, the idea of a necessary rule, repetitively applied to every chancy circumstance of time so as to give it the consistency of a narrative or a history. Once the name of this substitute providence has been chosen, the multiplicity of historical detail easily suffices, as we have seen, to discover in it a thousand verifications of its effectiveness. So conceived, history always verifies its law but never falsifies it; this is why, whether a good or a bad narrative, history will never attain science. In brief, it was a matter of continually composing a *Legend of the Centuries* – how should their duration be read? – in order to transform it into a tellable narrative.[3] And how are we to define a law of history except as a redundancy injected into so many circumstances?

Amid this repetitive desert, the prize for cleverness goes to Hegel's dialectic. Hegel didn't merely place the intersection of the Same and the Other (encountered in Lucretius, a materialist, as well as in Plato, an idealist, as much in astronomers as in theologians), whether gigantic or tiny, like his predecessors, at the origin of the world and once and for all, but set it out in detail, in small change, in order to reinstall it here, there, now, across all places and times, or, better, made it work locally to produce historical time. The marriage of chance (the antithesis of the thesis), of the negative (unhappiness and falsity), with necessity (the redundant thesis) is made *hic et nunc* while continually repeating itself in order to make these here-and-nows mobile. Next, in the sense of infinitesimal calculus, Hegel integrated the whole of these intersections, of these oppositions, of these avatars, of these pieces and local movements into a general picture-river. Had he read Laplace, Lagrange and the French mechanists of the eighteenth century, in particular Poinsot, the author of a theory of couples in which two forces are opposed in a simple and mobile schema, as with the philosopher, in order to explain every local movement, which are integrated to the point of placing, at the centre of the world, a universal couple that moves the world in its entirety? Local and global, the work of the negative functions in time the way this couple does in space.

In this series of translations of an initial model, can I find the beginnings of a solution to the question asked above? Yes, this progressive secularization of the prophetic kerygma erases divine presence so as to only preserve a design in various versions: the rational growth of the Enlightenment, the coming of the reign of

[3]See Chapter 2, note 8. 'Legend' here is meant in the sense of a map.

the mind, classless society, the victory of the proletariat, the rule of the market. . . . Again, can this express conception of a finality be put in brackets so as to only retain, ultimately, an integration, broad and flexible, of contingencies? Can chaotic phenomena be used as support, so to think – chaotic phenomena whose necessity is known when they are considered backwards and as past, but whose unpredictability, as well, is known for the future and forward?

In other words, a prophet announces a transcendent and necessary god, draws up his design, laments over the fortuitousness and chance of contingent detail and deplores the Evil to be combatted, which this divine design must triumph over. Only retaining, via a first filtering, the immanent portion of this inheritance, the philosophers of history I just spoke about, so christened by Voltaire in his *Essai sur les moeurs*, drew up, in their turn, a design, but a human and collective one, and therefore set forth a law that was just as necessary, one which would aid in combatting chance, error and Evil. Via a new filtering, we only retain, for our part, from this last inheritance, a rational necessity, one reread in the upstream direction but tied to improbable contingency and illegible downstream; we only retain the multiple outpourings of contingent narratives. In the end, we never stop asking, full of pathos, the question of Evil.

The sixth variation: The anthropology of religion

I admire the multiple avatars of a model that continually reappears and which we find again, now, no longer thrown all over the world, inside living things or launched like a motor of time and history, but at work in the secrecy of our bosoms, of our desires and of human hatreds, in the sacredness of cultures and the piety of religions, in the subjectiveness of consciousnesses and the collectiveness of groups, precisely regarding the question of Evil.

Where does its violence come from? René Girard asks. From imitation, he says. So again: from repetition, from redundancy, from the same. Why do women and men follow an intellectual or clothing trend? Why does voluntary obedience found powers? Why do we prostrate ourselves before society-determined greatness? Anthropological and tragic, Girard's model invites us to discover, first and foremost, the primary glue whose adherence forms a good portion of the social and personal bond: this imitation, whose gestures and behaviour, words and thoughts bring us closer to our cousins the apes, whether chimpanzees or bonobos, over whom, *Aristoteles dixit*, we win out in imitation.

Our desires ensue from imitation. Some person loves his friend's mistress or his mistress's friend; some other person is envious of his close neighbour's job. The state of being equals creates a rivalry, which, in return, transforms us into twins, arousing both hatred and attraction again. The entire landscape of violent feelings, of basic emotions, a landscape diverse and coloured in appearance, shoots forth from this uniform twinning. We desire the same, desire makes us the same, the same makes desire, which reproduces itself, monotonous, on the double map of Tender and Hate-filled. We imitate, we reproduce, we repeat. Replication spreads individual desire and collective cultures the way DNA genes reproduce and differentiate life.

This is one of the great secrets of culture, especially of the culture we are living in, because our big revolutions – carving stones during the Palaeolithic, writing in antiquity, printing during the Renaissance, assembly line industry for the last two centuries and the new technologies, more recently – all invented codings whose invasive superabundance characterizes our society of communication and advertising. These replicators, whose similarity arouses and reproduces the mimetism of our desires, seem to imitate, in their turn, the reproduction process of living DNA.

The main risk run by our children is this: we plunge them into a universe of replicated codes; we crush them with redundancy. The crisis of their education is this: founded on imitation, learning teaches to become inimitable singularities. The media, advertising, commerce, games, on the contrary, thunderingly repeat: imitate me, become automatic vehicles for the repetition of our brands so that your repeated gestures will multiply, by repeating them, our commercial successes. Shy, almost without voice in the face of these despots, education whispers: don't imitate anyone but yourself, become your freedom. Having become pedagogical, our society has therefore rendered education contradictory. Lastly, the crisis of creation is this: in a universe of replicators, of trends and of reproductive codes, of clones soon, inimitable works remain hidden up until the foundation of a new world. Via this mimetism, human culture amplifies or generalizes one of the secrets of life, which itself is always replicated.

Even though we don't have any words in our languages to say an object, a form, a human behaviour or even a word . . . endowed with, besides their utility, their meaning, their beauty, endowed additionally, as I was saying, with the power to replicate themselves, we never stop fabricating, conceiving and propagating them. Since we don't have this word, it must be invented. In the past, Plato constructed – and from start to finish – the word 'idea'; there is the idea of an object, of a form, of anything. All the beds in the world, the philosopher said, imitate the idea of Bed; all the circles in the world imitate the idea of Circle; better yet – he didn't say this, but I will repeat it – all the beds and all the circles in the world imitate or repeat each other. Formulated in Plato's fashion, the idea expresses everything except the strange motor that makes it reproduce itself in order to produce all the beds or all the circles in the world. The idea sculpts the idol without letting its power of replication be seen.

Why not say *ideme*? Many authors today, especially from the English language, and in reference to DNA and its selfish power of replication, propose to construct a *memetic* science, desperate nonetheless, they say, to discover a *meme* in order to take a picture of it. Of course, they won't manage to do this, as it has been a question, since the Platonists, of a universal operator (both theoretical and applied), of a model and of an image, that is to say, of an idea. Let's call idea 'ideme', a word indeed modelled on 'idea', of course, but also on the ending of *théorème* [theorem] or 'phoneme'; in addition, via its kinship with the Latin *idem*, it lets the strange dynamism of replication be seen that makes up the entire secret of its propagation. So repeated ever since, so commented on, so critiqued, praised or ridiculed, even become so common, Plato's idea ought already to have been called ideme. It would therefore present two components: its meaning, its content, its density, nay, its beauty, its inimitable character, its very universality, on the one side; on the other, its motor power of propagation, its imitable character, therefore a different universality, one bridging the inimitable and the imitable. Plunged amid an *idemalist* culture, we have a great deal of trouble distinguishing, in an ideme actually produced or uttered, its singular purity from its greedy and sometimes destructive capacity for invading space and time.

Once again, where do violence and Evil come from? From imitation, from the same, once again. The same rains down in the fields of desire, of money, of power and of glory; little love rains there. Imitation, sames or idemes rain down, the way, in the past, atoms, words or letters rained down in the emptiness for the foundation of the world. When everyone desires the same, the war of all against all flares up. We don't yet have anything to recount except this hate-filled envy on the part of the same that sets doubles and twins in opposition as enemy brothers. Semi-divinely performative, envy produces, in front of itself, endlessly, its own images in its likeness. The three Horatii resemble the triple Curiatii; the Montagues imitate the Capulets; Saint George and Saint Michael imitate the dragon; the axis of Good acts symmetrically to the axis of Evil, according to its hardly reversed image. Generalized in this way, covering all of space with imitation, conflict risks doing away with the warriors down to the last. Terrified of this possible eradication of the species by itself, all the belligerents turn, amid this crisis, against one. Mobs of humans kill the single human in a gesture that's repeated all the more since the murderers don't know what they are doing.

Then, but only then, does narrative begin: the one recounted by both the book of Judges (11.34-40) and the Greek tragedy, and the one, in my turn, lastly, I can tell. 'If I win this war', Jephthah, the general of the armies, beseeched, 'I shall offer the first person I meet as a burnt offering to the Lord.' 'If the winds rise again to turn my sails toward Troy', Agamemnon, the admiral of the fleet, prayed, 'I shall sacrifice, on Neptune's altars, the first person who comes toward me.' A fine breeze filled the sails of the Greek warships, and this father, the king of kings, saw his own daughter Iphigenia come towards him. The Jewish army crushed the sons of Ammon and, dancing and playing the tambourine to celebrate the victory, the daughter of Jephthah himself came out of his house, in Mizpah, running, joyous, towards her father, who was triumphant but was rending his clothes. Life, time, circumstances and history drew these first comers randomly. Sons and daughters, always children. The victim of violence seems to draw lots, but, always, the lot falls on the youngest, on the ship's boy, thus veiling the secret of war: the murder of descendants, whose organization, by these vile fathers, is hidden beneath the randomness.

In the dismal plains of the battles and squabbles of the same against the same, both of them desiring the same, and therefore without news or information, the most improbable of messages rises, then, and all the way to the heavens, at the height of the cruelty. The fathers become the worst fathers over the course of narratives in which the same, necessary, intersects death, randomly; an evil that appears in the same place as Eve's disobedience amid the redundant performative, as Lucretius's *clinamen* in the parallel rain of atoms, as the falsification of an experiment against a law's repetition, as mutation across replication, as the improbability of historical circumstances held in some stranglehold by a hand that's even said to be invisible. Anthropological and tragic, Girard's model varies, once again, on the invariance from just now: narrative becomes possible through the intervention of chance amid necessity.

The seventh variation: Literature

I am reading Ulysses's adventures on the divine sea. . . . Reaching this song, I still don't know whether he will shipwreck or put in at Ithaca and his wife. I am eager to know Jacques's loves, which are fatalistic and contingent, those, gloomy, of Madame Bovary . . . , the name of the murderer. The author of these narratives holds the first element, the universal law, in his hands like an omniscience or like absolute knowledge, while, as a reader, I move, blind, from episodes to peripeteias. Even when he plays at not knowing, the narrator knows; the listener journeys to the end of his night. The former sometimes condescends to share his knowledge with the latter, to suddenly present the Grand Minister of Finances to him as the very brother of these hungry poor people, come from afar, in Egypt, to seek out some grain to subsist, but then the characters themselves remain in ignorance. A necessary transcendence sees; incoherent immanence lives in front of a veil. The narrative's tension between these two poles, between these two roles, blind and seeing, chance and necessity, wherever they may be situated, installs a tear, an inspection hole, a viewing port, whose glow resembles the dawn of knowledge. The appetite for knowing goes, tense, through this opening installed between light and darkness, whose blinking, occultations and flashes guide, like a lighthouse, our wandering and its errors.

Not only does narrative constitute the *I* and the *we*, but it institutes subtle games, as exciting and as serious as those of hide and seek and blind man's buff, by which knowledge commences.

The universal passion of women and men for stories, that of children in the evening for tales of sorcerers and fairies, that of their parents caught up in a suspense thriller, that of an assembly faced with a skilful speaker, an eloquent orator, a theatre play, a cinema screen . . . , that's when a curiosity as burning as it is acute is aroused. Far from scorning it, the first chapter of a treatise on cognitive science should treat literature as an epistemogonic trap: false or true, I repeat, imaginary or real, wise or crazy, it makes no difference – narrative gives birth, via this opening, to the human craving for cognition. The author plays, in the sense of a game; the reader enjoys, in the sense of pleasure; the narrative puts some play, in the mechanical sense, between omniscience and these gropings. Together they imitate the real state of exact knowledge. Kill literature and your sociocultural tradition will no longer produce, in the end, scientists or science.

So let's reconsider literature by taking up the double thread of chance and necessity again. The development of an ancient epic, of a Greek, Renaissance or French seventeenth-century tragedy leads their characters, *volens nolens, invitus invitam*, towards a fate that's, in spite of everything and in spite of themselves, just as fatal. Achilles, Hippolytus or Phaedra, King Lear all run blindly towards a death that we fear but which we make out better than they do. Always, a clearer and sometimes necessary continuity agglomerates a thousand events of a group or a life, events which are ambiguous, partially sighted or heroic. Likewise, the intimate declarations of autobiographies indicate a line, signing at least the identity of the man or woman who is confessing and whose direction gives meaning and coherence to the circumstances recounted, to the obstacles encountered, to the scattered emotions, to the sometimes contradictory affects. Epics, histories, phenomenologies of mind, legends of the centuries, romance novels, swashbucklers, detective stories, theatrical action, film scenarios, representations in every sort of media . . ., what genre could do without this tension, destinal and cognitive, between a guiding thread unfolding semi-necessarily, like a movement with wind astern that impels forward, and a hundred stones met with by chance, over which one stumbles . . ., could lack this application, more or less successful, of the tangency of the stones onto the guiding thread, or of the latter onto the former? Circumstantial multiplicities, sometimes with opposite meanings, become oriented together, easily or with difficulty, according to this or that attraction. There can be no information without a channel, and no message on the channel all by itself. Otherwise, the pure multiplicity of grains would scatter into a chaos crackling like a background noise or into a violence without any rule; or, conversely, pure and simple repetition, uniform and sterile, would weary, would put to sleep, would even lose all meaning due to the very unicity of the direction, or would unfold into a uniform violence without any obstacle. Suspense is attached to the point of tangency of contingency, well named, to necessity.

Evil, reprise

Hence the use of Evil, which without fail tears up formal unity. How can we not be surprised at the fact that fine feelings or edifying stories make for such lousy, boring, stupid, even unintentionally comical narratives? The reason is found in the balance of the two elements forming the message. The Bible puts knowledge of Evil at the beginning of the story of history.[4] But, all things considered, every narrative requires an uncoupling from repetition, demands not only contingent circumstances but especially some event apt to break the monotony of necessity, rending the reign of its law. Suddenly, I regret repeating myself. I shall do it again, alas: there can be no narrative without redundancy, of course, no message

[4]The story of history = *l'histoire*. Later in this paragraph, the story of our history = *notre histoire*. As mentioned in Chapter 1, note 5, *histoire* can mean history or story. Both meanings seem to be at play in this paragraph.

without a channel, but there can be no narrative either without rupturing this same repetition. God speaks, and things appear, of course. But the first chapter of this Genesis would not be able to last. Beyond a week – I'm still repeating myself – this chapter would no longer give any information. Don't be shocked that biblical creation botched its job so quickly! With this redundant rhythm, its narrative speedily exhausts itself, which does nothing but endlessly repeat the divine word's performative: *fiat*, *fiat* . . ., an excellent channel, of course, but one quickly emptied. In comparison, the Grand Narrative lasts billions of years because, at least at its beginning, its message is jam-packed with different laws every millionth of a second. Rarity abounds in this case; in the previous case, chanted repetition reigns. But now speech, omniscient with redundancy, is going to lose, all of a sudden, its sovereign power: a woman rises up and gets around the prohibition. Yes, for any narrative to begin, a rare piece of information has to enter into its channel, a singularity has to rend its generality. There was only one law; a minimal grain breaks its line. Since the reign of necessity does have to be ruptured by a contingency for the story of our history to begin, Eve's deviation then (anti-law, counter-necessity . . .) becomes an element that's difficult to avoid in its economy. Better yet and quite precisely, it's a matter, in front of the serpent and under the apple tree, of the beginning of knowledge. I see here the original bifurcation, which the theory of narrative in fact renders inevitable. Disobeying becomes a major ingredient in every narrative as well as an awakening to knowledge.

Evil, in narrative, plays, as we have seen, a role parallel to falsification in scientific experiments. Do celestial mechanics, mathematical physics, astro- and geophysics, thermodynamics, biochemistry . . . proceed any differently, I mean according to different rules? Do they not apply this or that necessary law, mathematically formulated, to experiments of this world, themselves tied to singularities of time, of space, of motions and forces . . . such as the contingent existence of humans and things shows them? No science would do without this tension between a guiding thread following a necessary unfolding and a thousand grains of random states of affairs, without an application, exact or precise, of the former, mathematical, onto the latter, experimental. Multiple phenomena federate themselves according to these or those formal equations, successively written by Galileo, Newton, Dirac or Schrödinger. . . . There can be no knowledge of the world without these channels-laws; but there can be no exact science either without the multiple messaging of their concrete falsifications. We find again, in the sciences, the rupture of law, the fact that puts a grain or a thorn in the flat channel. Without this falsity, there can be no true science. Falsification opens up the second chapter of science, that of contingency, the way Eve's disobedience opens up the second chapter of Genesis, that of history. And, despite the distance between these two cultural zones, for similar reasons.

The final variations and the extreme edges of the spectrum

So now the announced spectrum is unfurled. At one of its extreme edges, even mathematics shows a rigorous battle between logicism or formalism and an abundant and refined proliferation of 'existents' that are hard, resistant, unexpected and perfectly 'real': for the history of its language is teeming with words that express these disquieting encounters with 'things' that don't submit easily to the preceding laws: irrationals, imaginaries . . . as though this history continually had to adapt its line to severe falsifications it didn't immediately know how to get around. It doesn't even know yet how the prime numbers are distributed in the smooth sequence of integers. Mathematicians find too many 'existents' of this type before them to agree to reduce their discipline to a pure channel or to the principle of identity, or even to the absurd idea that here it would only be a matter of conventions invented at leisure through our experience or our ideas. I remain a 'realist' because I have practised mathematics.

Conversely, and at the other extreme of the spectrum, with living things, since neither individuals nor species nor their environments repeat themselves, the biological sciences seek to minimize laws – one might think they were afraid of them – while maximizing circumstances and contingency. Except for the fact that, for several decades, the combinatorics of genes has precisely repeated few enough elements in the genetic code to again point towards universality.

Do practices like those of medicine or law proceed any differently? How many times, as a patient, have I failed to notice, as though in mutual examination, the double head of the person who was observing me to treat me, whose first two eyes were contemplating his knowledge of the disease with an entirely inward attention while the two other ones were acutely scrutinizing my singularity as a sick person? One gaze towards the necessary, the other towards the contingent. How many times, as a traveller of the West, have I failed to note the tension, modern and contemporary, between nations having Anglo-Saxon law, whose jurisprudence, quasi inductive, develops from case to case, and countries with Roman law, whose jurisdiction stems, almost deductively, from previously posited principles: more stable and necessary, the latter; more shifting and contingent, the former? If either should want to belittle the other, the one might mention the other's stiffness and the other might mention the first's cynicism; the faithfulness of the second or the adaptivity of the first, on the contrary, will be praised. The fact remains that in the two practices, centred on the body in pain or the contractual group, the same two elements – fluctuating circumstances and easy channel – are found.

No doubt a certain formal logic founded on the principle of identity, $A \equiv A$, no doubt a certain ontology, frantically repeating the essence of Being or the existence of beings . . . can be considered to be pure channels, infinitely tenuous, for the messages, sublime with emptiness, of a human language as stripped of information as apophatic theology, repeating just as frantically what God is not. No doubt, secretly, flaws are found in such discourses, no doubt, the incoherence of the words of an idiot, full of noise, sound and fury; no doubt, the hubbub made by cities, groups, thunderstorms, earthquakes and the sea can be considered to be the content, packed with nonsense, of an absence of message.

Narratives said to be literary – even religious, medical or juridical – or sciences said to be hard, even battle? In both cases, it's a matter of tying together, with more or less harmony or success, the one and the multiple, chance and necessity, the *τείνω* and the *τέμνω* of time, continuous extension and granular divisions. The guiding thread of a heroic story or of an innermost confession, the vocation, supposed or not, of a people or of a woman, the fatality of a destiny, irresistible loves, heart-rending separations, pitiless vengeances . . . follow a line that recruits, like a force field, scattered circumstances and random events without any other link than this guiding thread. But this tension between the continuousness of the thread and the discontinuity of the states of affairs is found again, almost as is, when we apply the rigorous laws of logic or mathematics to states of affairs dispersed in the luxurious detail of the world. This is the announced encyclopaedic spectrum, whose range unites, for the first time, hard sciences and literary narratives, always divorced on grounds of mutual fault.

So information theory would interpret this situation by saying that the law, that the necessary unity, that the common redundancy – forces, for example, whether strong or weak, are repeated everywhere in the universe – form the channel, as it were, of a message, whereas the multiplicities, unexpected and rare, of a world teeming like a horn of plenty constitute its content. It seems to me that Western culture often oscillated between the Plato of the mathematical forms and the Aristotle of the individual substances, between the Descartes of the entirely simple and easy chains of geometry and the multiple Leibniz of the infinite monads. Irresistibly drawn myself, at the start of my life, to the intoxicating formalism of mathematics, I am finishing my life amid the endless rejoicing of landscapes and of narratives of knowledge and of the universe, of humanity as a species and as an individual. I loved the purity of simple channels; I now enjoy being in front of the luxurious superabundance of detail. I will have spent my life at this wonder-filled wandering: traversing the spectrum I have just drawn.

Thus Narrative receives a new status, a cognitive value and a cognitive dignity. Rigorous proof lines up equations and constructs systems; the exact sciences describe points of tangency between theories and experiments; contingent knowledge is expressed in narratives. From the cosmogony that follows the evolution of the Universe to the evolutionism that relates the descent of the species and of humanity, all these sciences recount. Narrative becomes a canonic mode of knowledge. Lastly, the Grand Narrative integrates the entire spectrum unfurled in this way.

The new originality of the Grand Narrative

But the Grand Narrative goes beyond this spectrum. I can now understand and show, in comparison to this synthesis of traditional knowledge, always tied to a type of marriage between chance and necessity, that we can finally realize, as I was saying, the astonishing newness of the Grand Narrative, whose unfolding reverses the distinction that rules over the marriage, whose variation permits continuously traversing this spectrum. If, everywhere, contingencies are more or less subject to a necessity, conversely, in the Grand Narrative, necessities play the role of circumstances linked together contingently.

For what happens all along this global epic? With each bifurcation, a law, new and unpredictable, becomes grafted onto the preceding ones. It remains or becomes a law but forms a branching. It remains or becomes necessary but announces itself and starts out as contingent. In the case of every other narrative, an unexpected circumstance, a chance . . . open up a new branch, bring the new and the rare, that is to say, information, and are going to fight to accept or refuse entering under the common law, at least in order to inflect it, at most in order to change it. Here, on the contrary, a law, sometimes rigorous, plays this unpredictable role, brings rare information, creates a new branch. Even the Universe seems to begin contingently with the Big Bang and only finds rigorous laws after the Planck wall bifurcation; single-celled organisms spread the rules of life over an inanimate and blue planet, which therefore becomes green; *Homo sapiens* divides it up and exploits it systematically. . . . In redistributing, in its way, the classification of the sciences, the Grand Narrative makes them into a contingent Genesis. They quit the role of being a channel so as to take on the role of being information content.

How can this happen? I don't know, but I can venture a hypothesis. At least since Galileo, we have known that a change of scale imposes, in space, unexpected transformations. Of course, iron and cement and not only paper are necessary for a building several stories tall to stand, whereas its model makes do with cardboard; but also, the quantum laws of the microcosm differ from the laws that regulate the perceptible world, of human and astronomical dimensions. To quantitative variations in the dimensions of the expanse correspond drastic changes of nature and quality, and even diverse universal laws. At a large scale, here is an orbit or the harmony of lines of a map; at a small scale, there are Brownian motions, quantum jumps, white noise and the fractal; the statistical scale determines the law of large numbers; in detail, vagaries and brouhaha dominate. Must, at the vast scale of the

Grand Narrative, the line and the law themselves be drawn at random?

Must similar transformations be obligatory when we move from a few millennia to the billions of years of evolution unfolded by the Grand Narrative? How are we to model its entire duration on laws issuing from a time that's as minuscule as that of history – seven thousand years in comparison to millions – and on a percentage of information that would be so low, that of a few written human languages? Does this change of scale, concerning no longer space but time, change necessity into contingency? Does what appears necessary in the short term become contingent over an interminable duration? Darwinian laws, for example, have lasted for 3,800,000,000 years; they entered the fray, if I may, at the dawn of living beings but had remained unpredictable and unexpected in a universe in which only energy exchanges ruled, whether physical or chemical: compatible with these energy exchanges but not deducible from them. However hard Darwinian laws may present themselves as today, they came about contingently, and so as new. A certain order of reason has it that necessity wins out over contingency; we discover – and behold, no doubt, newness – that contingency can suddenly arise, entirely fragile, despite the omnipotence, crushing and redundant, of necessity.

I return to the subjective

To this new discovery, on the side of reason, is added a rejoicing, light and secret, on the side of existence and my joy. The Greek sea off Patmos; the vast high seas between the Galapagos and the Marquesas; the glaciers of Greenland towards the warmer zone where they calve; Ama Dablam, the Himalayan cylindrical summit, guardian of Everest; the end of the Andean summits in the vicinity of Patagonia; that aurora borealis in Montreal; some French landscape, green in Creuse, dry in Gascony, rocky in Brittany, vertical on the walls of the Alps . . . didn't quite give me the intense joy of their beauty because they could be deduced from the principles of geophysics, optics, electromagnetism or thermodynamics; and yet, they were deduced from them! Nonetheless, this necessity suddenly metamorphosed, in front of me, into an inimitable contingency, whose singular radiance illuminated, there, the present moment. I don't love you merely because I obey the laws of sexual begetting – I nonetheless submit to them – but because, in a rare circumstance, I encountered you, you, inimitable. Impelled by an irresistible vocation, my life is made up of a contingent sum of random appointments, including, sometimes, points of tangency with eternity. Does ecstasy not come about from the fact that *this* – fragile and shifting here and now – changes into necessary, or, via an equally miraculous reversal, from the fact that some implacable and redundant rule mutates into an immediate and rare dailiness? Fatality into freedom? One might say that these two categories of modality tremble, at the same time as my body and my soul, the one category transforming into the other and vice versa, at a dazzling speed.

By a similar vibration, you will recognize the true work of art: the contingent colours and forms in the chance hands of Manet or Soulages; the vernacular language under the quivering pens of Racine or Céline; the simple tones of Couperin or Fauré; the banal marble under the chisel of Houdon . . ., all of them suddenly became – miraculously? – as necessary as the constellations of the heavens. We workers on beauty have no mad dream other than to transform, by the magic wand of our fragile technique, our daily labour, as ordinary as the hour that passes, into a necessary work. The nothing, dense, exists! If I therefore know, from experience, to what extent the time of my existence is committed by this improbable hope, how much do I tremble with joy at seeing, towards the end of my days, and conversely, as it were, the entire Universe, known by me as well as by others for its implacable necessity, begin to sing, almost of itself, its metamorphosis into a contingent landscape, streaming with the time of a rare beauty. This is my last message.

Or it is this. Doesn't the intoxicating beauty of the vital, human and world adventure come from the fact that we never know if what we think, what we do, hope for or feel, here, now or even for a long time . . . is due to contingency or necessity; that we never know if, banal or decisive, our acts and thoughts commit us, and the world and the others, or don't have any weight or pertinence? Those, certainly, were landscapes, works and adventures whose chance illuminated my days; but these above all were people who, through the same metamorphosis, led me to the Third Heaven. Like the ecstasy of beauty, the transport of love changes law into event and event into law. Contingency and necessity transform into each other, in a vibration that makes us quiver with anxiety and elation.

Just as I surged up from a tentative narrative, just as we almost died from a history, short and mendacious, likewise, from this Grand Narrative, from this immense caduceus in which contingency and necessity are woven together, humanity and its humanism are finally being born today.

Subjective, collective, therefore relative

I began with Greece, mathematics and metaphysics. Deductive, demonstrative, formal, this declarative thought encounters, in front of it and in its own zone of validity, the step by step of algorithms. At this crossroads, revived today by computers and biochemistry, I deviated from the global to local detail, from schema to landscape, from figures to fullness, from the necessary to the contingent. Thus, I carried out my pilgrimage to the east, from Athens to Jerusalem, from *logos* to *muthos*, from Euclid to the Bible, from Plato to the

Gospels, in short, from the cognitive and objective universal of being and of the concept to the human, subjective and collective universal of the narrative. But this voyage had begun with Lucretius and *Rome*.

From the ancient Latins all the way up to the modern Christians, the Eternal City never stopped working on the synthesis between stories and forms. Rome united Athens and Jerusalem. In the same way that Cicero or Lucretius had translated the Greek philosophers into a language that's more capable of recounting Livy-style narratives, Saint Thomas Aquinas united reason and tradition, demonstration and jurisprudence; Descartes staged his *Meditations*; the Age of Enlightenment combined the *Encyclopedia* with *Jacques the Fatalist* and the *Confessions*. Literature haunts deduction.

A passable mathematician, I have just recounted narratives. Without them, reason wouldn't be enough, and without reason, narrative wouldn't be worth anything. Narrative repays reason, which gives the weight of truth to narrative, with access to everyone. Their grafting becomes universal without enslaving. Pedagogical and cognitive, the bridge between the pure sciences and literature broadens to the point of expressing here the Semito-Indo-European catholicity of the West. This is my oblique way of attaining the Grand Narrative. I am not claiming that its universality can only be reached by these paths; I am only unveiling them in order to confess their relativity. Thus, this book runs from my humble wandering to my relative belongingness and from this latter to the hoped-for omnitude. I invite my friends from other cultures to open up their own path towards this universality, where I shall make, this morning, an appointment to meet them.

We no longer recognize ourselves in the various broadenings of our national or linguistic collectives into cultures or civilizations. Our time of hominescence poses questions and constructs objects such that the humankind announced by this time no longer stitches the today to histories that are extremely short and dispersed, but to the common Grand Narrative. We had recently left it; we are taking it up again.

THREE NARRATIVES OF HOMINIZATION

The Bible: The Hebraic version

At the beginning, I recounted how, with at least three reprises, human groups separated. I am returning to my start. I shall invent again: a tale, if you will, a myth, a history, a true knowledge, assuredly a narrative. Here it is. Among the abominable pirates and brave people who left Africa and abandoned each other cheerfully, nonetheless with tears and sobs in their throats, a small team, maybe even a single couple, at the end of a wandering whose length I shall never know, reached, by chance, to the east of Eden, not far from the Persian Gulf, an islet, between two rivers, without any predators.

Such an environment can present itself contingently. I have known, on the Garonne, an island-paradise where I only perceived the sky; a plant collector on Lake Bienne, Rousseau described a similar island; fairly recently, the convicts abandoned there colonized an empty island since called Reunion; hardly seven centuries ago, a deafening symphony of birds, flying in thousands of species, blinding with their luxurious hues, some of them delicious of flesh, greeted the first Maoris on a deserted New Zealand . . .; Jules Verne and Robinson didn't recount nothing but twaddle. Scattered over every latitude, blessed isolates could be discovered. So I am repeating, while generalizing it, a story, invariant across its variations, that could have happened to any group wandering across the world, whether remaining in its neighbourhood or travelling the open sea.

So having arrived there, in a nest between two arms, Euphrates or Ganges, Orinoco or Congo . . . , the aforementioned couple didn't find crocodiles or sabretoothed tigers, dangerous insects or deadly germs; rather, they found a mild climate, fruit trees in abundance, non-polluted springs, prey that allowed itself to be caught. Let's stop, they said. Since life expectancy increases with an opportune life, they gave themselves over to the innocent delights of love and language, named the animals and plants, adored, knew a little.

What happened in this chanced-upon paradise that left nothing to be desired? The soft origin of a hardness? Amid the trees with fruit that's good to eat, Genesis says that a woman, Eve, one of these hunter-gatherers, whose existence we know about today and whose wandering I have just followed, fell. How? I believe, for my part, that, a genius, she glimpsed the laws that govern life; life, I mean flora and fauna, plants and animals, the serpent and the apple tree. That she made out their cruelty. That she wanted to turn away from them. That she saw that, all the same, we could never do so. That she discovered that life, implying death and therefore crime, lived in a state of sin.

Before this first-principle moment, the couple in question, but also their predecessors for millions of years, ancestors who hardly count since they hadn't discovered the secret of hominity, these two humans, as I was saying, about whom I want to recount, in my turn, how and why we are right to call them our first parents, were participating, on the island of Eden like everywhere else, simply, natively, carnally, wildly, archaically, originally, naturally, vitally, supralapsarily . . . in this primitive existence in which, hunting down and being hunted down as well and like them, the wolf eats the lamb, in which the condor carries off the goat, in which the tigress hunts the gazelle . . . without any compunction, in which the laws of the jungle require tearing limb from limb in order to eat or dying as prey and food, killing the male rival in order to couple with a female in his stead, devouring the young of this female so that she will come back into heat, in which, without being aware of the laws, perfectly Darwinian, of adaptation, of selection, of the success of the fittest, of the multiplication of descendants, each living thing adopts these laws in the purest innocence. At the beginning, we lived under these laws, animals and humans from before the human. The state of nature political philosophers referred to and evolutionary nature such as the neo-Darwinians describe it can be seen unfurled in Ngorongoro Crater, across the Australian Outback . . . Edens whose gardens are perpetuated before our eyes, territories where impeccable killers tear each other apart.

Finally, a woman we agree to call Eve came along. In a revelation that could be called transcendent – and I don't see how, admiring its genius, it could be named any differently – she became aware of these terrifying laws, of the crime hidden within innocence. She could no longer endure this paradise, this nature, this state, this evolutionary time, in which death makes life live, in which continued life necessitates the death that one deals out. Hominization begins with this intuition, this revelation, this fall; you should understand by this that melancholic, desperate, tragic recognition of the inevitable horror of the laws that govern less the state of nature – an idiotic oxymoron presupposing the static stability of a state that never took place or time, whereas we live in the continuous disequilibrium of what never ceases being born – than natural evolution. Disgusted with killing, crying out in pain before the necessities that let living things survive, faced with the obligation to submit to them, suddenly nourishing the mad hope of disobeying them, humanity, in her, through her, after her, abruptly bifurcated.

I dream that Eve dreamed as Isaiah did:

> the wolf will live with the lamb; the leopard will lie down with the goat. The calf, the lion cub and the fatling will go about together; and a little child will lead them. The cow and the bear will graze; their young will lie down together. The lion will eat straw like the ox. The nursing child will play in the asp's den; the weaned child will put his hand on the viper's hole. They will no longer cause hurt or violence on all my holy mountain. (Isa. 11:6-9)

Eve dreams of this second innocence because she finds the first one to be criminal: the one in which the living thing, heterotrophic, finds itself required, in order to eat another living thing, to first put it to death. In order not to kill any animals, Eve contents herself with eating the apple. Thus, she loses the innocence of the other living things, impeccable murderers.

Inside the very heart of life, Eden contained Evil, bound to she who knew it. Just as a branch shoots out from a trunk, the human leaves natural and deadly norms when it becomes aware of the abominable laws of brutal life. It emerges from hating the death and violence that the struggle to live carries inside itself. Our mother had the transcendent courage to approach the vicinity of this bright and burning fire, the delicious apple and the repugnant serpent. I kill to eat; everybody seeks to kill me to take my sustenance, my females and my place; I find myself required to yield to these laws, natural, but find them to be atrocious and conceive of them, when I submit to them, either as a perverse pleasure or as a nauseating disgust and, then, as an ineffaceable guilt . . . desire for the apple, serpent's poison. Humanity, in us as in me, is born from the leap out of innocence, out of the nakedness of impeccable killers: is born from this Evil that didn't exist before humanity recognized it.

I am recounting here, once again, a narrative. A true one? Did this story of Eve take place and time? Once or a thousand times, yesterday, thousands or millions of years ago, here or elsewhere?

No one bears witness to it; I have only heard it read or recited. I don't claim it to be history, as is said, nor exact experiment, even less logical rigour. Yet its narrative rings true: dense with meaning, it emanates from a deep knowledge, from the incontestable certainty in us that never stops concerning life: we know life to be lovable and hateful, good and criminal, soft and hard, beautiful and hideous, innocent, culpable, exhilarating, devastating. We let ourselves go with its necessary laws and so judge our actions to be repugnant. Can I rewrite Genesis into Darwinian language? Yes. It doesn't matter who bears the name of Eve, the heroine of the narrative; you, me, we, woman or male, finding sin in innocence. Can I claim my narrative to be true? Lively, exciting, above all heuristic, it opens up the way to seeking further.

Thus I can no longer help but believe in original sin, so much have wars and murders crisscrossed my life, my memories of existence and of history, my culture, so much have a hundred slaughters made us know the perennial abomination, no longer of the state of nature, no longer only of Darwinian evolution, but of the violent history that, by always bearing its trace, remains in the state of this sin. Just think about how many people claim to be hominian and nevertheless enjoy killing each other while pretending to believe that these slaughters were necessary, occasionally without having any need to eat. I believe in original sin, in the reproduction, incessantly present, of its violence. This sin puts a permanent obstacle in the way of the process of hominization, but, at the same time, it allows it a continual resumption, so much does this sin instigate the fight that has to be unceasingly conducted in order to distance its terror, always returning. I believe, in addition, I can call it original because, from it, the hominian arose: from taking upon itself the guilt of the laws, innocent and Darwinian, of life; from suffering from dying; from being ashamed to kill; from knowing all the same that one cannot live without eating, therefore without putting to death, without loving, therefore without risking refusal, therefore without having a rival, therefore without the danger of murder . . ., lastly, from knowing that it could never again live without tears. Thus it was born inconsolable. Our exploits (from thus knowing the rules of selection, Abel invented livestock breeding and Cain agriculture) and our inexhaustible tears (murder was nonetheless repeated between these brothers) flow from the source that is original sin. We cannot console ourselves over the fact that the second prophetic dream of innocence will never come about. I hear Eve shaking with sobs, like me.

So, kicked out of Eden, quitting both innocences forever, the criminal one, in fact, and the peaceful one, in dream, the human, with the same heart, loved life and detested it. This love-hate for nature and life expelled us from paradise. This is the hominian bifurcation: fall and expulsion, the fall from the height of animal unconsciousness, the expulsion from nature's evolution, in which one kills without any compunction. Our species' branch bifurcates starting from this deviation from nature and the laws of life. From the point we became aware of the death implied by life and its bloody slaughters, we lost innocence. The original sin, which we cannot help but to believe in, so much is it repeated over the course of our history (so accommodating in relating violence, so persuasive in finding it to be necessary), so much is it repeated over the course of time, in collective relations, in the very inwardness of our consciousness, the sin of violence lies at the very root of the impeccable life. This life compels eating, reproducing, evolving, therefore dying and killing, at least killing in order not to die. I have before me, as a more than true object, incontestable, as a problem, more than insoluble, as an emotion, more than deeply distressing, this mixture of horror and attraction; we have as our horizon love-hate and life-death. The first knowledge, prior to truth, there it is, on the tree with the bifurcations. Darwin himself knew this knowledge and, before it, was also troubled.

I conjugated the preceding page as much as I liked by freely mixing several subjects – I, you, we and humankind – as first persons. A subjective, collective, cognitive and objective narrative. Who today would, for example, have the audacity or the naiveté to claim that humanity was born good and that society had perverted it? I don't believe in my native goodness, nor, pardon me, in yours, even if I love you, for I have heard the genius of your furies; no one believes any longer in the goodness of any collective (cite a single society that has managed to maintain its history without crimes?) nor in the goodness of humanity in general (except in the goodness of those innocent supralapsarian murderers, who didn't know what they were doing . . .) so as to make the wickedness of some individual or the wickedness of society responsible for Evil, even though human relations combine and multiply the wickedness that howls in each of us. So I don't believe that Evil comes from one of the subjects, I, you, he, we, the plural you, to the exclusion of the others, innocent, nor, at the limit, that it comes from everyone. Nor from the devil to the exclusion of God. Nor from God. It comes from life.

In the past and recently, philosophers constructed a tribunal in order to make this person or that person appear before it, responsible for Evil. As for me, I don't find any subject to be guilty. Or, in a way, I find, as for me, every subject to be guilty, including me, since every subject was born from guilt, from the evident knowledge of the first state of innocence as being a criminal state. I believe Evil to be objective. It issues from life, from evolution, from biological laws, from the selection called natural, from the constant death implied by the perpetuation of living beings. Like the rain, the wind, the snow, the storm and the summer heat, life and its laws remain innocent, in the Garden of Eden as well as in the Gobi Desert, as long as they don't encounter some subject, knowing Eve, for example, a subject born from this encounter and from the burst of love and the gasp of horror she or this subject experiences in the face of life and its laws. I therefore believe Evil to be objective, subjective and cognitive. This newborn subject no longer wants to die or kill; it must nonetheless do so if it wants to survive. It recoils appalled before these contradictions, before this chance and this necessity.

This recoil, this deviation, this fall, this expulsion from innocence, this is the hominian branch, the hominian bifurcation. The individual, the group, the species, I, we, everyone . . . are born, here, human. Of necessity, I have to, we have to continually negotiate with violence and death, just like every living thing in this world, but I cry, we moan, I twist with pain, we howl with guilt . . . from doing so: humankind is born from doing violence and from doing violence to itself. The subject was born from that. You shall no longer kill. Faced with the Evil of living, plunged, hands and feet bound, in wickedness, in the maliciousness of living, universal humanity began, in all the islets-Edens spread from the Euphrates to the Garonne and from the Ganges to the Orinoco, with this double suffering lived in real time by both the individual and the collective. It arises from the anguishes of the *I*, the *you* and the *we*.

Furthermore, faced with this new subject, the object, literally human again, also comes from death, whether received or given. The deviation from the law of life, of course, forges the subject when the living thing accomplishes this deviation, and this subject forges the object, since, facing me, facing us, facing humanity, lies the first object, a nameless corpse.

I need to clarify this deviation, which scriptural tradition describes as a fall or original sin. This bifurcation distances humans from the innocence of plants and animals. Mustn't we see the patent fact that we accept scientific Darwinism and reject social Darwinism with horror as proof that we discern, with as much disgust as clarity, the deviation-opened gap that separates the necessary law that enslaves life from freedom, life-saving and fragile, and from human history? No, we will not submit to the laws of the jungle.

But why say fall since, on the contrary, said sin provoked humankind to go outside the bestial, whereas said innocence delivers the plain and the forest to every cruelty, to the bath of animals in blood? Because in deviating away from pure slaughter, the culture that was brought about by the fall described this murder as impure. Eve found the law of mutual murder to be unclean. Humanity was born from soiled death. The human arose from finding itself dirtied by death, infected by violence. I'm not saying that culture will never see murder, but at least killing will pose a question to it; who, then, will pose it? God, no doubt, for God said: Cain, where is your brother Abel? A response will be required; who will have to respond? The word 'responsibility' comes from this question. We find ourselves, in this sense, responsible for Evil, since only our eye, only our newborn soul saw and read this Evil in the innocence of the soulless and gazeless killers.

This deviation, this bifurcation took place, is always taking place, here and now, under an emotion that overturns like a groundswell. It falls onto my belly as it does onto Eve's uterus. This emotional tempest is necessary for hominization to begin, for subjects to form, objects to be forged, objects whose relations will develop and give birth to knowledge. This emotion, next to which any other passion seems cold to me, will develop and give birth to sadistic pleasures, to supernatural pities, to cruelties unheard of in the animal world, to charities the state of innocence didn't know in the slightest degree. Humankind will metamorphose into an abominable tyrant and a gentle humanitarian; it will run about in bands of pirates and mendicant orders, will live torturing sex and sublime loves, will suffer the tragic mixture of Good and Evil, so often indissoluble. The most refined knowledge doesn't save us from these atrocities, since they are formed and forged together. The permanent motor of our development remains this deviation from evolution we must never stop carrying out, this abandonment to the deadly laws of life, an abandonment plunged in a horrified refusal to follow them: cultures are constructed from continually negotiating the originary and unspeakable mixture of atrocious violence and universal love.

The process of hominization, to become clearer, only has need of Darwinian laws and their sudden reversal of direction in the gestures of a subject, a subject born all of a sudden upon the knowledge of their cruelty, born all of a sudden from the awareness of their abomination. The Grand Narrative recounts the bifurcation of our branch, but many religious narratives also tell this and attempt to give a reason for it. The fact that some religions were horrified, in their turn, for a moment at these laws is easily understood, since humanity, as I cannot stop repeating, was born from separating itself from them while obeying them, since humanity is forever being born from the pain it feels from them. Humanity deviates from evolution. Darwin himself thought so, noted it, knew it, maintained it, moaned over it. Without this deviation, the hominian couldn't have been born; it couldn't have had knowledge; it couldn't have sinned or taken pity. I separate myself from the laws of life; therefore I am in despair and shudder with joy. I abandon the laws of life; therefore, free, I act and choose. I deviate from the laws of life; therefore I think and know. At the beginning and in continuous time, action and thought are mixed indistinctly with this deeply distressing affect. They are founded on it. I will die disconsolate from this.

In listing off a few episodes, such as the Garden of Eden, the fall and the expulsion, the murder of Abel by Cain . . ., Genesis recounts, in a refined and forceful way, this brutal deviation with respect to evolutionary laws, which made us into the humans we never stop becoming. Religious narrative comes closer to science and its Grand Narrative than it is believed to, and when religion is set in opposition to Darwinism, both of them are unaware that they each confirm the other. These struggles excite the stupidest of those who prefer conflict to thought, who prefer anger to invention.

By opposing the laws of life, humanity is born, also, the knower of these laws. Desirous of tearing itself away from the rules of the jungle, humanity ends up knowing the Darwinian laws of evolution. We carry the laws of Darwinian innocence on our shoulders; we obey them, but with such shame, such guilt, that we abruptly bifurcate from five or seven vital kingdoms. We will never again live as innocent living creatures. Social Darwinism would lead us back to the animal innocence of monsters athirst for blood; applied, social Darwinism would hurl humanity, now equipped with global weapons, into eradication. If we reduced the gap of our deviation, if we returned to the laws of life, for example to eugenics, we would not survive; for innocence presupposes ignorance. We can no longer not know; knowledge becomes the human condition. Let's lastly recognize how close the roots of knowledge are to the roots of Evil.

The fall or the deviation opens up a space outside of life, called by ten names: collective, for cultures; subjective, for consciousness; cognitive, for the mind and knowledge; objective, for science . . . or, as well: thought, freedom, humanism, ethics, spirituality . . .. The name of this new world matters little; it's simply a matter of seeing it open up, of holding it open. I sometimes fear that it is closing, so much do we suffer the delightful temptation to return to the laws of life, to fall back into them, to plunge back into them, to let ourselves go with them. Every morning we have to recommence the process of hominization, the opening of the deviation. Yes, in real time, we have to quit life while remaining in it, hate life while continuing to love it, continually negotiate a bittersweet, ecstatic and painful mixture of murder and cooking, of laughter and tears, of violence and dearly acquired peace, of innocent savagery and refined culture, one of the two attractors distancing us from the other, but which is always plunged in its counterpart.

A second stage dates from the Neolithic and even from today, the stage of auto-evolution: our modest contemporary mastery of the laws of mutation follows directly from the other modest mastery of selective laws through agriculture and livestock breeding: Cain, a farmer, and Abel, a shepherd . . . together represent this beginning, before today's taking over of the reins. Not only do we know how to recount the Grand Narrative, but, knowing the double dynamic of evolution, we act on selection and mutation. Going beyond history, once more put between brackets, we re-establish ties with the Neolithic, with that origin I am reciting.

In a certain way, we are repeating, here as well, the beginning of hominization I have just tried to describe, whose ancient date rings, as though in harmony, with this date, distant and near at the same time. By means of a tremendous loop, we are returning to the beginning, when unimaginable ancestors achieved this deviation from evolution, leading us to maintain this deviation, even though our fate would remain bound to its laws. For today, re-establishing contact with the ancestral gestures of the inventors of agriculture and livestock breeding, we are completing, by grasping mutation, their grasp on selection. Becoming humans, we had quit evolution, while remaining glued to it; we are quitting it a second time, by objectivizing it into technologies. Second generation, our genetics revisits Genesis.

Genetically modified organisms (GMOs), cloning, nanobiotechnologies, the dangers of eugenics . . . arouse anxieties as deep and strong as the emotion that accompanies original sin. Let's have the courage for this comparison: we are bringing knowledge and violence into the processes of birth. Once again, the origin of humanity, the origin of living things and their ramified evolution are at stake. We are deviating, a second time, from natural evolution, from a 'natural' way of being born; we are quitting reproductive innocence, the random lottery of 'nature', of million-year-old traditions. Will our successors later say that today we too had left paradise?

Already distanced from the blood spilt by the deaths brought about by selection, hunting, rutting and competition, perceiving this blood to be criminal and the one who shed it to be sinful, today we are distancing ourselves, by manipulating mutation, from the ties of blood and its genealogical lineages; we are all gradually becoming adoptive parents.

Humanism assumes that we know humanity. We can now recount it, first. We easily recite its African origin, its adventures in the entire world, its various habitats. But we aren't merely making literature; we are also analysing and can combine the elements that constitute humanity. We know how to answer twice, in narratives and in equations, the question 'where do we come from?'

If 'nature' signifies what is going to be born, then we can, for the first time, say that we know human nature. We know it both in the time of the evolutionary narrative as well as in the time of its constitution. We know where humanity was born, where it departed from, when and how it left this cradle, where it passed through, where it was headed, where it set up its home: the first narrative, the grand one, about which I said, as a Preface, a few fragments. I have just recounted here how, starting from the very laws of evolution, humanity became the humanity we know. I would willingly call my narrative irenic, capable of bringing peace into useless battles.

But moreover we know, and practically, what elements humanity was constituted and developed from, like every living being: a narrative that's other and same, that of the hardest sciences. Thanks to this, we can finally lay our hands on these elements. And if knowing means being able to change, we can finally change it if we want to. We can make humanity be born just like any living thing. We made it be born the first time, as paleoanthropologists recount it; we made it be born a second time when we tore it away from evolution; we can make it be born today, a third time. It will perhaps be born from this new power and the problems it poses, from the deviation we will take on in the face of this possibility. We know, I repeat, human nature in the sense where this word 'nature' designates birth: we were born from a DNA mutation; we were born in Africa; we were born, in Eden, from suffering and refusing the violence required by life; we were born from culture and speaking; we were born from knowledge and free will; we are perhaps going to be born from technology.

For all these reasons, humanism has just been born. I repeat, going back beyond the history that teaches us almost nothing useful about this question, humanism brings us back to all our origins: our biochemical origin, our paleoanthropological origin, our evolutionary origin, our technological origin . . ., 'natural' and cultural origins. This doesn't mean happiness on earth, but the opening of a new conquest, of a new struggle against a strange future, as strange as the one that opened up to Lucy or one of her equals; as the one that opened up to Eve and Adam when their first deviation caused them to leave their paradise of criminal and 'natural' innocence so as to launch themselves into an unknown and free world; as strange as the one that opened up before Abel and Cain, the saint and the murderer, when they had mastered, for the first time, natural selection through agriculture and livestock breeding.

We don't know where we are going, but, for the first time, we truly know where we came from and sometimes why. We at least hold a knowledge whose assurance allows us to predict that violence and death will never cease to accompany us on this new, difficult-to-open-up path between and against violence and death towards life and peace.

Fables: The Greek version

With wind astern and a fine sea, they were sailing in long stages in the middle of the *Mare Internum* when, one ordinary morning, the lookout announced land dead ahead. Ulysses, the skipper couldn't believe his eyes or ears, no experienced pilot having ever reported an island in these waters. Yet, a rocky spur was trembling, beneath the sun, at the horizon. Bracing the sails aback and letting the ship move under its own momentum, they dropped anchor in a cove with black sand. The crew descended onto land to explore, under the supervision of the ship's officers.

The island belonged to a woman, Circe, an enchantress, who bore the name of the falcon that wheels above its prey in circles, as in a cirque. She received them in her residence and, to welcome their arrival, offered them a drink with a strange taste. Even though, as he was recounting his travels to uninhabited lands, Ulysses drank some, he remained stable in his human form – Hermes had given him a remedy that would protect him from any poison – while his sailors, under the effects of a potion that made them dizzy, were being transformed into pigs.

Thus sings the *Odyssey*. But Homer didn't understand very well and didn't finish the narrative. La Fontaine took it up again and continued it by drawing a second circle. So Ulysses was bragging about his exploits while his sailors, under the effects of a poison that made them dizzy, were being transformed, his *Fable* says, one into a gull, another into a snake, this one into a wolf, that one into a roaring lion; an entire menagerie suddenly escaped from the residence and invaded the island, the water and the air. The pigpen had turned into a zoo. Each of them grappled with his own animal.

Ulysses remained just as he was. Tall in size, wide of shoulders, a good storyteller with a fertile tongue and radiant eyes, he began to delight the solitary woman. Over the course of the nights that followed, he even showed himself to be an accommodating lover. The enchantress was enchanted with this companionship and little by little dreamed of no longer being without it. As crafty as a Greek, he guessed this. And, on one of those sweet nights in which the lovers became intoxicated with dialogues and caresses, he ended up confessing to the mistress of enchantments that he was bored stiff with his companions and wanted to see them return to their original human shape. Enamoured, she accepted, but on condition that Ulysses ask them if they themselves wanted the metamorphosis to be reversed, in short, that the decision be freely made.

So Ulysses undertook to go see the lion, who answered him:

> You're kidding. The king of all living things, without rival or predator, I devour whomever I like; I launch my lionesses hunting; everything that moves bows before my claws and worries at my roars. Why would I allow myself to be

> transformed back into an obedient bos'n, risking being punished with running the gantlet, sleeping poorly, fed poorly, a servant?

Likewise, he went to consult with the gull, who answered him: 'You're joking. I fly, consider the land and beaches from on high, haunt the ultimate zones of the air, feed myself at will on things that swim, while enjoying diving like lightning onto my prey. Can you believe that I would ever accept to become a slave again, hoisting the sail at the whistle?' Thus he went and questioned the stag, who answered him: 'You must be jesting. I dominate the woods of my forests and ten does with my sex; I rove the thickets; sometimes I even happen, fleet of foot, to leave the packs of dogs slavering at my heels in the dust. No, the wild life makes me happier than shipboard seasickness.' Thus the skipper wore himself out, in as many ways, in proposing the same liberation to the spider, the boar, the viper, the carp and even the earthworm . . .; all of them, without exception, answered that they'd prefer to remain as they were. Alone, he returned to Circe's residence, vexed. She laughed.

La Fontaine, aged, stopped there, understood a little, but he didn't finish the story either. Of course, from having absorbed Circe's potion, the sailors had turned, in his work, into cicada and ant, wolf and lamb, lion and gnat. . . . In his turn, and even more of an enchanter than the enchantress, he metamorphosed Homer's pigs into all the animals of Aesop's *Fables* as well as his own *Fables*. His quasi last poem, in the last book, the twelfth, in which he varies on the Homeric story in this way, seems to draw its moral from his prior *Fables* by showing with what enchanted ease humans descend into the skin of animals, but how poorly, on the contrary, they extricate themselves from this species envelope. Look at how right I am, he seems to say, in addressing myself to your common nature of being fox, heron, stork or dove rather than to your rarity of being human! Your freedom would consist in extricating yourself from this ever-so-shared animality, in finally freeing yourself from my *Fables*.

Since he didn't say this, I shall continue the narrative by drawing a third circle in order to try to finish it in his stead. So, laughing, Circe said to her vexed lover:

> To metamorphose your sailors into animals, they hardly had need of being pushed; they would have returned to this of themselves by their own wish, as it were. No secret is hidden in my potion; you could have given them pure water, and the drinkers would just as quickly have become shark, frog, bear, vulture or wolf. It is sometimes enough to wait: time and age transform them in that way. They grow old dingoes; they die peacocks.

Ashamed of seeming to moralize, the enchantress stopped a discourse whose cynicism was separating her from the arms of her lover, who was pensive. In the luminous night and in front of the infinitely smiling bitter sea, Ulysses had, for the first time, understood this strange episode of his *Odyssey*: as in the Game of the Goose, his vessel had just sunk, with all hands, into the common well of animality. Did his crew and he have to start over from scratch, begin the game of life and evolution again? He had gauged the irresistible animal attraction that reverses our wandering towards humanity, which denies, checks and impedes the advances of pedagogy whose lines he had written on the divine waves.

I shall stress this: with a gigantic weight, the living flesh's memory energetically leads us millions of years backwards; we easily climb back down the tree of species from which we had emerged with difficulty. Whoever is lucky enough to live as a human often dies as a dry insect or a money-grubbing leech; each of us dies from our own animal. But the direct metamorphosis, the becoming-human starting from the animal, what an ascesis, what an ascent! In a life, how can one succeed in retraveling, for oneself, the path of hominization, which, over millions of years, had traversed hunting and violence, hunger and desert, sea and thirst, sweat and plowing, exercise and the swimming pool, courage and the construction site, learning, school, intelligence and science . . . plus adaptation to the other, in bed? Who wouldn't prefer to receive, once and for all, claws and fangs, innocence and dominance, seasons assigned for lovemaking?

Yes, the legend of Ulysses and his companions, fallen into the well of animals and so intelligently varied by La Fontaine in his fable, even if this latter didn't quite finish it, finds, here and lastly, a major fragment of the Grand Narrative, which, itself, precedes it, extends it, gives it meaning and follows it: read in this story, astonishingly preserved from age to age, from the French language to Greek and from writing to oral tradition, the long and difficult patience of hominization; gauge how much our deliverance cost with respect to the evolutionary origins and the lightning-fast freeness of the fall back down. How useless and harmful this verb 'being' shows itself to be in the question – what is humankind? – since we continually advance towards it, painfully, and continually fall back, suddenly and with a cheerful will, towards the animal.

An abrupt bifurcation is making me take a tangent in finishing: if every fetish shows how a man or a woman fights, victoriously or in vain, to emerge from the animal that's intimately mixed with his or her body, this story recounts the entirety of wordless fetishisms, which are as below.

Fetishes: The version before any writing

A feathered serpent with the face of an old man, does Quetzalcoatl express, before our Darwinians did, the idea that birds came from reptiles and that *sapiens* evolved afterwards? In a single block, does this chimera amalgamate a time-counter of species? Does the Aztec pyramid erect in this way a temporal scale, a summation of evolution? Does this vertical shooting up of the lively in its long duration show, here, in devastated Tenochtitlan, that independent of us, the civilizations that we destroyed knew evolutionary life better and before we did?

Lying flat on its stomach with its four limbs tucked up, here is the bull; how can this land animal equip itself, for its part as well, with a bearded patriarch's head? By making wings grow from its back. That way it can fly, by degrees, towards the temple, cross its threshold, ascend to the altar and, contemplative, metamorphose into *sapiens* or sage. *Introibo ad altare Dei*.[1] In front of the Mesopotamian ziggurats, the ancestor of cherubim, this *kerubh* with three bodies – quadruped, bird and human – statufies in immobility the same evolution: in order to go from hooves to thought, two wings at least are required; in order to transmute a bovid into a meditative sage, the eagle must be passed through. So, like it, you and I, transported by the air above its gate, shall go into its temple to adore the Eternal. Since this chimera, for its part as well, guards access to a sacred site, we didn't hesitate, yesterday and yesteryear, to decipher its meaning by means of religious images, religious interpretations, religious symbols. . . . And we spoke blindly of fetishism, polytheism, idols, as in Quetzalcoatl's case.

Did we know clearly what we were saying?

Recent, these two evolutionary representations recall an older art on cave walls: in the Upper Palaeolithic, around twenty thousand years ago, the famous Sorcerer of the Cave of the Trois-Frères, in Ariège, France, already bore a reindeer's head; in Lascaux, Cro-Magnons painted, in the Shaft Scene, another human body having the head and beak of a bird. The engravings from southern Africa that represent similar doubles, half-human and half-animal, date back, for their part, thirty thousand years. Of course, we don't

[1] I shall go into the altar of God. Psalm 42.

know how to interpret such enigmas: symbols or rites? But do we understand the Aztecs or Assyrians any better?

Let the perspective be reversed: instead of recounting that some religion, fetishistic, polytheistic, pagan, what have you, venerates these mixtures of animals and human, respects them, prays to them (I repeat, who truly understands these assertions?), I am saying that these statues immobilize the evolution of animals into humans and that this process of hominization passes through the religious.

Does fetishism venerate chimeras? From not understanding a thing about this question and not knowing how to give it a response, I prefer to advance that such-and-such religion may allow the evolution, represented in this way, from the brute to the human. For these statues don't guard or crown a political, judicial or theatrical edifice but rather a construction where the sacred gives the meaning of actions and behaviour. Whoever enters Lascaux immediately feels the deep emotion induced by the temple, respectable, of an unknown religion; certain paleontologists call it the Sistine Chapel of prehistory. Does the metamorphosis represented here lead towards piety? The latter, quite the contrary, becomes a means, the motor, the condition for the metamorphosis.

So, yes, the serpent is covered with feathers before this winged creature, a vertebrate, becomes hominized, and the bull becomes an eagle so that this quadruped, mammalian, can become humanized. And these two transformations only take place there, on, in front of or in a temple. They don't go towards the sacred; rather, the sacred makes them possible. Without the religious, the evolutionary passage from the animal to the human couldn't have taken place. We have known this at least since the Cro-Magnons. In any case, this is the effigy, real and concrete, immobile and statufied, of the process of hominization. These animals evolve towards their head.

In the West as in the East, independently, pyramids, temples, access stairs, statues and tabernacles . . . climb towards the vertical with an eye to commemorating the greatest event that had ever taken place and time, for us, on this planet. How did a bull, serpent, winged creature or eagle. . ., a bird, a stag . . . slowly evolve towards sapience?

No, the riddle of the Sphinx hasn't given up its secret yet. We only know half of it. For the narrative says that Oedipus answered 'man' to the monster's triple question that asked: What animal has four, two and three feet in succession? The same narrative adds that after this solution the Sphinx killed herself and that Oedipus went on towards his fate. We stupidly repeat the word 'man' and believe, like him, that we have the solution. But why would the chimera commit suicide?

The riddle's definitive code resides in the narrative itself, which goes from the questioning animal, half-human but close to its death, towards this survivor, departing on a new foot, detached from his animal half, single, finally unglued. What should we call this movement from the animal death to the exclusively human departure if not a freeing, if not hominization? The double fetish has just given birth to the human. After this birth, it expires and disappears.

From mute statuary representations, speech was extracted; yes, this told narrative of the encounter between Oedipus and the Sphinx, which simulates, recounts, summarizes, displays, commemorates and encourages the passage between the biped and the four-footed Sphinx animal, his Darwinian ancestor; man comes from it, is born from it, frees itself from it. And here is another side of the secret: this narrative, mythical, is bathed in the religious, at least such an archaic sacred that death cannot leave it.

Just as, in La Fontaine, 'The Wolf and the Dog' recounts the process of domestication (how, from predator to parasite, did *Canis lupus* become *Canis latrans*?), likewise, the half-animal half-human double fetishes recount the process of hominization. In the latter, the animal and human remained glued together; in the former, two bifurcating animals detach themselves and run separately, the way Oedipus freed himself from the Sphinx. Profane and chatty, the fable follows the statuary and religious mute myth. Domestication dates from a more recent epoch than hominization. Far from believing the word of the loquacious animals of the *Fables* or looking at fetish images and fetish statues, I see them all evolving in cross dissolves. It's less a question of gods than of the process made possible by an ecstasy.

These chimeras show the hard and progressive exit from the state of being an animal. We could only extract ourselves from this state under costly conditions. Emerging slowly, the human remains glued to the animal. Alas, we still resemble the Sphinx, the feathered serpent, the *kerubh*-bull, the talking animals of fables, those living things with horns or bird beaks painted during caveman times . . . instead of the Theban hero. The composite fetish gods of Charles de Brosses, the crossbred monsters of ancient Egypt, all those chimeras of Assyria or Mexico, the deeply moving apparitions of Lascaux . . . therefore celebrate, often before writing, in an atmosphere of sacredness, the operation of unshackling by which we left and continually leave species. They show, in effigy, the origin of the despecies. How could and how can we still detach these bonds or dissolve this being glued together? With the help of the religious? Do we fall back into it without the religious? How do we break our chains of bones, of cartilages, of reflexes, of programming, of genetic automaticity? Did the religious deprogram us? Did its flame make us into incandescents?

Slow and gradual, the break with the animal world and, more generally, with the natural world, followed by the entry into cultural possibilities, in fact concerns the programme. The bond of a living creature with the things of the world depends on its specialization, on its differentiation. We became cultural as soon as we lightened this determination. We unbound ourselves, we deprogrammed ourselves. The genetic automaton slid towards learning. This process started from the animal world, hence the long being glued together. Still undergoing hominization, even undergoing auto-evolution, we never stop despecializing ourselves, dedifferentiating ourselves, whitening ourselves, incandescent. Some given species chooses some given detail in the environment and acquires perfectly adapted functions there, which, as though in return, allow it to choose this detail even better. Breaking this bolted-on bond quits this circumstance for the whole. The plant or animal chooses from among the things of the world. Universalizing, humankind grafts itself to the world.

We never stop whitening; not yet incandescent, always a little dirty, dun-coloured even, we never cease doing this progressive laundering, chaotically punctuated with backslides into the manure pit. Bulls, we try to detach ourselves from grass and the red fury; serpents, from our venoms; eagles, from our lambs, and the three from fleeces, scales, feathers, horns, beaks. Detached from animals, we still live with them and outside of them; they haunt us even though we try to live elsewhere. Our skin undresses itself of its body hair, our mouth removes the gag of its fangs, our hand removes the glove of its claws; we continue to toss off our juvenile clothes so as to flay ourselves living, like the victims of Xipe Totec.

Look, in passing, at how, again, starting from this same origin, technological objects set sail from the body, part after part. Garments, here: the horrible Aztec sacrifice scalps the human victim, and the priest puts on this mask or helmet; he flays him and covers himself with his skin as a robe. Moving on to animal sacrifice, Hercules likewise carves up the hide of the Nemean Lion; dressed in a skin that instils fear, he passes for being strong and terrible, a fetish or leonine statue, to the blindness of imbeciles, for we know him to be naked underneath, like everyone. This flaying divestment towards incandescence produces hominization at the same time as technologies, here vestimentary, theatrical or of masquerade. The human neverendingly strips itself. Technologies ensue from this same setting sail. The entire body itself can exit one's own body in its entirety in the form of statues. How could I have failed to see, in the past, this artistic process of exiting? We exit from fetishes; fetishes exit from us.

We didn't stand up all at once; we didn't talk overnight; we didn't fabricate tools on the spot; we even waited millions of years to attain cave wall paintings, geometry, a knowledge of life; we still live far from wisdom; which of us knows love? But we brought ourselves, but we are bringing ourselves into the world, or the world came and is coming to us in its globality: less mourning for the other than death; less these rocks than the object; less today than time and you than the other; less here than the horizon . . . in short, the deeply moving totality. Whereas species remain in their difference, our genus became hominized by opening itself up, ecstatically, to the universal, even though it exploded into cultural subfamilies. We devoted ourselves to these arts, those tools, that language by tearing ourselves away from animal specialities starting from this ecstasy.

Hominization has need of it in real time, every day and at this very instant. The liberation of the human animal won't continue without this ecstasy. It goes hand in glove with the religious, which will only be erased on the phenomenal morning we become humans, finally. Not anytime soon. My culture's religion calls this terminal instant: resurrection of the flesh. Then, under the tremulations of cymbals and the burstings of trumpets, we shall become humans, entering into our glorious bodies, freed from the apocalyptic swarming of animals.

When, among his readers, publishers or translators, an author seeks a reputation for seriousness and honesty, he multiplies, in his works, footnotes at the bottom of every page and appends to them, at the end, an enormous bibliography equipped with an index.

But, for many years, it has been enough to call up any word of any book on a search engine to receive, on the net, every possible bit of information in the world about every question connected to them. The internet forms the sum of all possible notes and substitutes for them.

Over the course of your travels, you have observed a hundred times that hotels ask their guests to conserve towels for praiseworthy ecological reasons. By referring to this integral of all documentation and by doing without this advertising, I am trying, as I have ever since I began writing, to conserve paper.